D.A.R.E.

*Real Strength
for dealing with
life's challenges*

Tony Bellizzi

D.A.R.E.
A process for dealing with life's challenges

Copyright 2013   Tilt publishing   printed by Unitech
First Edition: 2013
Second Edition: 2015

ISBN: 978-0-9856909-2-2
Tony Bellizzi

D.A.R.E. is dedicated to the Holy Family: Our Lord Jesus Christ, Mother Mary, and St. Joseph and to all the young people I have been blessed to meet in communities, churches, schools and jails around the world.

All profits from the sales of this book will benefit the Hope for the Children Foundation and their work with at-risk youth.
visit : HopefortheChildren.org

Special thanks to 2nd edition editor Shara Berkowitz

Table of Contents

	Page
Introduction	6
Part 1 Life Challenges	
Addiction	15
Alcohol	16
Anger	20
Attitude	21
Betrayal	22

	Page
Body Image	24
Bullying / Cruelty	25
Burying Feelings	26
Conflict/Drama	27
Cutting/ Self-harm	29
Death	30
Depression /Anxiety	32
Divorce	34
Drugs	38
Eating Disorders	40
Emotional Pain	40
Failure	41
Family Challenges	42
Friendship Challenges	44
Friends with Challenges	46
Gangs	47
Guilt and Shame	48
Hopelessness	49
Jealousy	49
Loneliness	50
Money Challenges	52
Moving	53
Parent Conflicts & Challenges	53
Peer Pressure	57
Physical Challenges	58
Poor Self Image/Insecurity	59
Prison	63
Regret	64
Relationships	64
Running Away	66
School Challenges	66

Sex	67
Sexual abuse/Rape	71
Sibling Challenges	72
Sickness	73
Smoking	74
Stress/Pressure	75
Stuck	76
Suicide	77
Violence	82

Part 2 Faith questions

Afterlife	84
Changing the World	86
Church concerns	86
Doubt	88
Faith	91
Following God	93
Forgiveness	94
Life	96
Life Mission	97
Love	99
Mary	99
Morality	100
Occult	100
Other Religions	100
Prayer	102
Priorities	103
Sacraments	105
Suffering	106
Conclusion	110
Parents and Adults	112

By My Side

Where are you going?
Can you take me with you?
For my hand is cold
And needs warmth
Where are you going?
Far beyond where the horizon lies
Where the horizon lies
And the land sinks into mellow blueness
Oh please, take me with you
Let me skip the road with you
I can dare myself
I'll put a pebble in my shoe
And watch me walk (watch me walk)
I can walk, I can walk!
I shall call the pebble Dare
We will walk, we will talk together
We will talk About walking
Dare shall be carried
And when we both have had enough
I will take him from my shoe, singing
"Meet your new road!"

Then I'll take your hand
Finally glad
That I am here
By your side
By my side

from "Godspell" by Stephen Schwartz

Introduction

What you are reading right now is a guaranteed process of dealing with the things that life can throw at you. DARE is a tool kit to help you move forward to a new and better life with a spiritual foundation, and practical common sense methods. It may be the only book of its kind that dares to put God at the center of the process of facing life's challenges.

It's a process that is simple; but not easy.

DARE is a guidebook for personal and social healing, and transformation. It can save and change lives. No matter what challenge you are going through in life, whether it is included in this book or not- *follow this simple plan*:

D don't ignore or cover it up
A always go through it with God
R remember to get help if you need it
E everything can be handled

D don't ignore or cover it up

Face the fact that change, and pain come into *every* life. Yours will not be the exception. Situations, groups and individuals are guaranteed to come into your life that will challenge your state of well-being.

It's what you do with them that matters.

Don't ignore reality, pretending a challenge doesn't exist or is not important. Don't be afraid to go through your pain. Resist the temptation rampant in modern society to dull the pain, to numb yourself from all that hurts in this life.

Ironically, many of the challenges covered in this book are the result of the choice to cover up something that is painful with a short-term solution to take the pain away. Then the second choice makes things worse, even becoming a greater challenge than the original.

Accept that challenges will always be part of life; because the more you try to escape from the challenges of human life, the more you are bound to them. Some will be difficult, others painful, some will seem overwhelming; but all of them are an invitation, an open door to growth. Looking back after you have changed for the better, many of your life's experiences will be seen by you from your new perspective to have been a gift.

A always go through it with God

The biggest lie of our time is that there is no creating God; and that we are all cosmic accidents. This is bizarre since it is science that is actually providing us with the most compelling evidence of an intelligent creator. For example, the entire universe is expanding at the exactly perfect rate; just slightly more or less, and it would not exist. Most astrophysicists refuse to believe that this is a random coincidence.

As an extension of there being no God, there are the additional lies that it is possible to live a good, full and happy life without faith; and also that it is possible to get through life's challenges and hurts without the assistance of a loving and all-powerful God.

Many people reject God; because to acknowledge Him is to admit vulnerability and need, and maybe even have to admit and repent doing wrong. No one likes to admit they don't have it all together; and no one likes to admit that they were wrong.

Do not go through life challenges alone. Nothing will happen in your life that you and God cannot handle together. These painful, upsetting events are not signs that God has abandoned you. You may be even tempted to blame God for what is happening to you. It might not be so bad if, out of frustration, you have a blow-up; but don't shut out your heart from the love of God that makes all things new. God is ready to help you get through whatever it is that you are facing.

No matter what it is that you're dealing with:
-Pray for the strength to act; to dare to do what it takes to move forward, and for the courage to forgive.
-Have the guts to be sorry for the mistakes and sins you have made. Remember that we live in an ocean of mercy and we are to extend that mercy to others.
-Remember that when we say forgive, we are not saying that what was done to us was OK.

Offering it up means that in enduring what you are going through, you are lifting up that pain to God for the good of others in need. Doing this powerfully brings goodness into the physical and spiritual world.

Bring it to **God**- no matter how big or how small. The only hurt He cannot heal is the one you do not tell Him about. Not that he doesn't know about it until then; it's that He will not intrude in our lives. We give Him permission to enter or not.

R remember to get help if you need it

Start with someone you trust- someone who is a good listener and will not judge you; and give you good spiritual and practical advice.

Sometimes we need to talk with someone who knows more about how to deal with our situation than our trusted friends and family. This means talking with a counselor if necessary. If you have been seriously wounded, if you, or someone you care about, are seriously struck, it can be helpful to speak with someone who has more knowledge than you, and can help you through the process.
Even though a good counselor, social worker, or other professional person may not have all the answers, they will know which questions to ask to help you figure some things out that you had been stuck on.

Bring Jesus into the counseling process with you since many professionals do not have a Catholic, Christian or even spiritual outlook. Stay away from any professional who:
1- wants to prescribe medication without listening to you.
2- wants to stretch out the counseling process forever.
3- belittles you.
4- lacks the specific expertise in the area you are dealing with.

Do not go to a psychiatrist as your first choice. Many prescribe medication very freely; and while some people need medication, a lot of people can figure things out without it. Go to a counselor first and together you, your parents, the counselor, and Jesus can figure out if you need a psychiatrist and/or medication.

E everything can be handled

Again, nothing is ever going to happen to you in this life that you and Jesus can't handle together. At times it might appear that a situation is unbearable or impossible- so remember those words. Labeling is very important. The words we use, the labels we give to situations, determine how we will feel about them. This, in turn, determines how we will respond to them.

If there is one thing you are definitely NOT going to find in this book it's the word "problem." I refer to all the situations in this book as challenges; opportunities for growth. You label something a "Problem" you respond one way. You label it a "challenge," you feel and act another way.

> *"Life is a mystery to be lived; not a problem to be solved."*

(Personally, I think I would have done so much better in Math in school if "Math Problems" had been called "Math challenges" or "Math opportunities.")

Personally, I am not a professional counselor, therapist or psychiatrist. When it comes to the most serious of the challenges included here, I have consulted people who know more than I do.

The method I present here, I have used myself, and it has been tested by many adults and young people my work brings me in contact with. I have never had any desire to write an advice book; but in my spiritual work with young people on retreats and in prison, I always keep things real. It is important to focus on turning to God for healing not only for our deepest pain but also the struggles and challenges of everyday life. Then we must go go forward to make specific changes.

This is a simple approach, but I am not saying that the challenges people go through are easy. Real growth takes time.

Real Strength

Becoming and being a strong person is never easy, and *ultimately this is a book about strength.* This is the simplest book you will ever read about strength; something that everyone wants.

All our lives we see people all around us trying to be strong in ignorant ways:

1- **Violence against others-** Trying to make ourselves feel strong by making someone else feel weak. The forms this takes can be: bullying, manipulating relationships, becoming a control freak, or hurting someone else. Using your power to build yourself up by dragging someone else down, so that they won't dare attack you is the most ignorant of solutions because you become a perpetrator of violence, and lose your ability to be close to others.

2-**Violence against yourself**-Shutting down our emotions; believing that if we do that we will never feel the ones that make us feel weak. The danger of this solution is that we end up killing off all the other emotions as well, and we never feel joy, passion, or inspiration either. You isolate yourself from your own self; from your own rich inner life, and you die inside.

3- **Ego trips**- Acting like you're better than everyone else. Puffing yourself up; strutting around, being condescending, putting up such a front that no one will dare attack you. You end up isolating yourself from intimacy.

4- **Escape-** Getting drunk, or stoned or acting like everything is a big joke or nothing matters or exists outside our mind-control device and virtual presence. Drugs and alcohol give the feeling of invincibility, and you feel immune from pain. They give the illusion that everything is just fine because they dull the pain.

The relief is temporary, and can become an addiction leading to challenges far worse than the original thing you were running away from.

The way to true strength is surprising:
> ***it is to admit where you are weak.***

Let God love you right there;
> and then His love becomes your real strength.

In this book we apply the DARE method to specific challenges. The foundation of this method is prayer; specifically the Serenity prayer:

> ***"Lord grant me the serenity (peace)***
> ***to accept the things I cannot change.***
> ***The courage to change the things I can;***
> ***and the wisdom to know the difference."***

*For some of the situations in this book, nothing can be done about them; and so the prayer is to accept.

*For others, action can be taken, and then the prayer is for the courage to act.

*Still others will require a combination of the two; with some aspects having to be accepted, and others changed

or

first attempting to change, and then having to accept if those actions do not work out.

This prayer is such a crucial understanding needed for life.
So much pain results when we try to change things we should accept, or accept things we should try to change.

The truth is: there is an amazing amount of love in our world. We are made by a Creator who has made us out of love. We are saved by a Redeemer, Jesus, who gave His life for us, and continues to pour out His love for our growth and healing. We are guided by a Holy Spirit who is present in our lives with many gifts including the wisdom, knowledge, and understanding to face our life's and our world's challenges.

The Label

Again, never underestimate the power of labeling in determining our experience of life. In my presentations I often include videos of young people, who have lived this; overcoming great obstacles to lead remarkable lives.

Jen Bricker was born with no legs, yet went on to play softball and basketball, and become a champion gymnast.

Nico Calabria is an exceptional young man, who was born with no right hip and leg, yet dives, plays volleyball, wrestles and plays soccer. His soccer goal is the most watched You-Tube soccer goal video. He climbed Kilimanjaro, as a Confirmation challenge; and is the one-legged person to have achieved this.

Victor in Peru, born with no arms and one leg, yet he walks, runs, plays soccer, does his homework with a pencil between his toes and goes on the computer and DJ's with an ipod, spinning the wheel with his big toe to select the songs he wants.

Jen, Nico and Victor all refused to label themselves handicapped. Their combination of faith, determination and God-given gifts led to their accomplishments. With their words, and more importantly with their actions, they demonstrate the strength this book is about. They reveal it is not just human determination; but faith that helps them make so much out of lives, that could have been so much less.

It IS possible to not allow the circumstances of life dictate how alive you will be.
This kind of strength is available to you!

I do not pretend to know everything. So if your experience in life has shown you something that needs to be added or altered, please feel free to contact me.

Where did the questions and topics in this book come from?
Every single question or situation presented here is exactly as written by middle and high school teens on my retreats. If on a retreat, the sharing is not coming out in the open, I give everyone who would like, a chance to share anonymously on paper what is on their minds, and going on in their lives.
     I have gone through thousands of these papers and index cards to put this booklet together. Not one has been made up, every single one is from the lives of actual teenagers.

Love is the answer;
no matter what is the question.

Life Challenges

Addiction
-*I'm addicted to pot & porn.*
-*I am addicted to video games.*
-*I smoke and I drink and I don't want to stop, but I am losing two of my best friends because of it. How can I make everyone happy?*
-*My friend is bulimic, and cuts herself, and is just not the same anymore. How do I cope with this?*
-*My father is gambling away a lot of our money online, and at casinos. My parents are fighting now about financial worries because of it.*

There are many forms of addiction, and certain families and family members will be more attracted to some, more than others.

In life, there are things that we *have* to do on a regular basis: eat, sleep, excrete, work, bathe and groom. There are things that many human beings *enjoy* doing: recreating, experiences of an altered state in sex or through substances consumed, playing games.   *And then there are addictions.*

It is important to know how your brain works. There is a saying "the neurons that fire together, wire together." This means that there are parts of the brain, that when they become used to being stimulated together, they will become strengthened; and this is how addictions form.

How do you know when you have moved into the world of addiction? An addiction is when a person does not feel fully alive unless they are engaged in a particular behavior, or with a particular substance. Using this definition you can see how many people are really addicted. The United Nations studies everything going on on the planet, and has determined that at least 1/3 of the human race is addicted to something. Some addictions include: work, gambling, smoking, alcohol, caffeine, nicotine. Some addictions are so rampant among the young that I deal with them specifically in this book.

Remember that the addiction, especially drugs or alcohol, will not help you deal with whatever it is that's going on. They might distract you from or take away the pain while you are high, but make things worse when you come down. If you can't stop, it's time to get help.

If it's YOU:
In general what you need to do:
1- admit that you are addicted
2- admit that you need God- pray
3- get support of loved ones and friends
4- seek ongoing support and advice from those who have recovered from the same thing you have become addicted to- hotlines, AA, NA groups in your town

If it is someone you care about:
1- speak with them (when they are in their right mind)
2- pray for them
3- if they are in deep trouble, make sure someone who can do more than you can is involved
4-consider an intervention (see alcohol)

Alcohol
-Ever since a serious incident, I have been drinking my problems away.
-My friend drinks. How can I help?
-My friends are all drinking, and I do not want to. How do I stay strong?

-My friend is an alcoholic, and won't listen to me.
-My mother was an alcoholic and then stopped, and now started again. It only lasted a day, but now I'm scared she'll become an alcoholic again. It kills me inside
-My mother used to come home drunk late every night. I would stay up all night worrying about her. Since then I have never felt the same way toward her.
-My family drinks a lot of alcohol- my father/mother is an alcoholic & won't stop.
-My mom is drinking a lot and smoking cigarettes- should I say something?

-I hate my father for things he did and said when he was drunk
-I love my brother, but he drinks and is violent.

Some people can take or leave alcohol; for others, their body will crave it in an addictive manner. For some people alcohol will be a big distraction; for others it will be a great destruction. For some it will simply be a waste of a great amount of money, time and energy in their high school, college and young adult years; for others it is the way they go down.

It has been scientifically proven that the alcoholic tendency is genetic, so look at your relatives, parents, grandparents, uncles, etc. If you have watched adults in the family struggle with alcohol issues, even if they no longer drink, the chances are very good that you may have inherited the tendency (males 90%). Does this mean you have to resign yourself to living life as a drunk? Absolutely not. It means it will be an issue for you; and you owe it to yourself to be careful.
Don't think you don't have to be careful if your parents don't drink. Some alcoholics get that way from peer pressure, or drinking to 'fit in' even though there's no alcohol problem in the family.

If you are wondering if you might be an alcoholic, these are the signs:
-Have you ever felt you should cut down on your drinking?
-Have people annoyed you by criticizing your drinking?
-Have you ever felt bad or guilty about your drinking?
-Have you ever had a drink first thing in the morning to steady your nerves or to get rid of a hangover ?

One "yes" response suggests a possible alcohol problem. If you responded "yes" to more than one question, it is highly likely that an addiction exists.
If someone you care about is addicted to alcohol:
1- *Recognize reality.* Do not play make-believe. Alcoholism does not just go away. Left on their own, the alcoholic's drinking gets worse and worse, as they need more and more alcohol to get the same effect. Brain cells start to die. The person makes bad decisions (85% of everyone in jail was drunk or stoned when they did what they did). They are responsible for their actions, but technically they weren't thinking straight. This does not mean that everyone who drinks alcohol will end up in jail. It means that people make a lot of stupid decisions while under the influence of alcohol.
2- *Take action:* Do not be an enabler, especially if the person gets violent when they drink. An enabler is somebody, usually spouses, friends, and family members, who make it easy for the alcoholic to keep drinking. They do things like cover for the person, or making everything nice all around them so the drunk's actions won't be so bad.
- *Speak with them* -when they are sober- do not waste your time when they're drunk

- *An intervention.* Talk to a school counselor or substance-abuse counselor about conducting an intervention. An intervention is when everyone who loves the person sits down with them together, expresses their love, and also their insistence that there is something wrong, and that they must get help. Don't try to organize it by yourself. If possible, ask everyone else affected by the drinking to join with you.

The reason interventions can be so effective is because when an individual speaks to the alcoholic they can turn around and twist it into it not being *their* concern. This is because only one person is saying something. When everyone in their life is united, they have nowhere to hide. The intervention should include a treatment plan. Detox and rehab is sometimes needed if the person is drinking so much that stopping on his/her own would be dangerous. Ongoing AA meetings are crucial for most recovering alcoholics.

(If you are the person with the alcohol problem take these action steps yourself. Dry out at a rehab is necessary. Get support. Join AA & get a sponsor.)

3-*Pray* for them, the change you wish for them happens first on a spiritual level, and through your prayers, you are part of their healing and recovery.

4-*Remember* that nobody changes until they are ready to change within themselves. Some people feel that because alcohol is a legal drug; that they should be left alone, especially if they are able to keep it together during the day and hold down a job. So if your efforts to help do not seem to be working, pray all the more.

5- *Get Support.* If you are a teenager dealing with an alcoholic parent or family member, find and join an Alateen group; where others who are your age can give you support and good advice. If you are an adult, join an Alanon Group or Codependents Anonymous.

Anger

-There is an uncontrollable rage growing inside me.
-I fantasize about killing my father who makes everyone's life miserable. His constant rage is destroying us.
-My cousin, who is like a sister to me, was in an accident and nobody stopped to help, and that would have saved her.
-How can I stop letting my anger get the best of me?
-How do you deal with feelings of anger and hate that even God cannot make you forgive?
-My friend blows up all the time, over-reacting, yelling for no reason

Anger is a natural human emotion to feel and is usually a secondary emotion. That means it comes about as a result of another emotion felt first; usually fear, pain, or frustration.
These emotions are normal, and sometimes even healthy to feel.
Some tips:
1-Take a timeout- pray
2-Once you're calm and thinking clearly, express your frustration in an assertive, but non-confrontational, way. Express your concerns and needs clearly and directly, without hurting others or trying to control them.
3-Get some exercise. Physical activity provides an outlet for your emotions, especially if you're about to erupt. If you feel your anger escalating, go for a brisk walk or run, or spend some time doing other favorite physical activities. Physical activity stimulates various brain chemicals, that can leave you feeling happier and more relaxed than you were before you worked out.
4-Think before you speak. In the heat of the moment, it's easy to say something you'll later regret. Take a few moments to collect your thoughts before saying anything and allow others involved in the situation to do the same.

5-Identify possible solutions. Instead of focusing on what made you mad, work on resolving the issue. Remind yourself that anger won't fix anything, and might only make it worse.
6-Avoid criticizing or placing blame. Be respectful and specific.
7-Don't hold a grudge. Forgiveness is powerful. If you allow anger and other negative feelings to rule you, you might find yourself swallowed up by your own bitterness and resentment. But if you can forgive someone who angered you, you might both learn from the situation. It's unrealistic to expect everyone to behave exactly as you want them to at all times.
8-Use humor to release tension
9-Practice relaxation skills like deep-breathing exercises, imagining a relaxing scene, listening to music, or writing in a journal
10-Seek help if your anger seems out of control, or causes you to do things you regret, or hurts those around you. You might consider an anger management class or counseling.

With professional help, you can identify what triggers your anger, and explore underlying feelings, like depression, fear, and frustration.

Attitude
-How do I get all the negative things people around me do and say out of my head and feel better?
-How can I be more positive & less negative?

Attitude is a choice. While you may not be able to control a lot, or even most of what happens to you in life; you can always control how you label those experiences. That label will determine the attitude you have about them, will determine your actions, and can carry over into your entire life. If you automatically label everything in a negative way, and it affects how you handle the situation; you may be stuck. It would benefit you to talk with someone about what you've been through;

what might be the original hurt that caused you to view things negatively, and how you have since put the pieces together in such a way that you, more often than not, believe that the world, life, other people, and even yourself, are not a gift.

Work on cultivating an attitude of gratitude; appreciating and being thankful for the good things in your life and stop taking them for granted.

-How can I accept people for who they are and stop judging people, when I have done it all my life?

This is an important question and a valuable goal to change yourself in this way. Simply judgment, while useful at times to insure your survival; more often than not becomes an obstacle and replacement for loving. St Teresa of Calcutta said, "if you judge people, you have no time left to love them." Pray to God for the help to see things the way He does; to see with His eyes. God looks upon all His children with love, not condemnation.

You can change this habit; even though you've done it a long time. Change is possible. Do it today. Don't wait until your judging, and refusing to accept, really hurts someone.

Betrayal

-A person I considered my best friend spread rumors about me and I can't stop crying.
-I've been betrayed so many times I don't know who to trust anymore.
-When everyone is against you, do you stay true or fade away?
-My friends talk about me behind my back.
-My friends have betrayed me. I still hang with them, but I feel like an inconvenience. Will I ever belong?
-I was stabbed in the back by my best friend.
-Some people I used to talk to treat me like a stranger now
-My school counselor was nice to me, now I find out he's a child abuser

Betrayal is an ugly, shocking thing to
Unhelpful reactions can range beating yourse
known better that the person would do that t
people out for good. Your brain will try to prot
ing stabbed in the back again by convincing you
of protection. "No one will ever do that to me agaii
That wall seems like a good idea at the time; but eventually it gets thicker and thicker, until true closeness between you and others becomes impossible. Do not give into this temptation. Accept that while ugly, betrayal is a part of life, (Even Jesus was betrayed) and you *will* get through it.

Pray about whether you should give the person another chance or need to walk away. Talk with them about the betrayal, and its impact on you. If you can tell that they are truly sorry, then give them another chance. If they do not care, or this is not the first time, then by all means let them go with love. If it is a family member, it may be harder to completely walk away, but you can maintain healthy boundaries. If it's family, unless it is regarding violence or abuse, you probably want to make an extra effort to forgive, since family is a web of many people connected to you.

No matter what, forgive the betrayer. No one but God is perfect. Let go of any bitterness or resentment. Not forgiving is like drinking poison, and expecting the other person to die. Remember that forgiveness is not saying that what they did to you was OK. It's saying that you are not going to hold onto it; you are going to let God take care of them. As long as you hold on, you are still allowing their hurtful action to control you. Choose the path of freedom, and remember what Jesus told us to do: to love even our enemies- this means praying for them, and for the best for them. Avoid the temptation to punish them by cursing them or badmouthing them or worse- plotting and getting revenge. Not much will kill your soul more than that.

age
...ve become very insecure about my body.
-How are girls supposed to be comfortable with who they are, and believe God made them in his image, when society constantly shows & tells them that they do not live up to their standards.
-I hate myself. I'm insecure about my appearance and ashamed of my body; the way I look, feel, my whole way of being.

There is so much pressure on women of all ages, and now even guys, to focus on their physical appearance alone. Obsession with body image is something that affects a lot of people. We live in a superficial society with a tremendous amount of focus on appearances. The images put forth by the society are not realistic, and often not even real. We are bombarded with models and celebrities; and many of them have had work done. Everywhere images have been air-brushed.

You cannot allow any of that to control how you see and feel about yourself. Enjoy being as attractive as you wish; but never let it consume or define you. Decide to accept and respect the body that you have been given; with all its positive attributes and imperfections. God gave you this body because he thought you might enjoy being in it.

Stop comparing yourself to others.

Decide if there are changes you can make- need to lose some weight? You can do that.

Your nose, eye color? Accept them. Plastic surgery in an age where people are dying from starvation is not morally acceptable- period. Before you get a cosmetic procedure done- I recommend you visit Smile train, which helps children born with a cleft lip condition. Imagine what their lives are like. Send them the money to have the procedure done. They're the ones who really NEED a procedure.

Bullying/ Cruelty
-I am made fun of for being fat, what I wear, how I look, what I do & who I'm friends with.
-Rumors have been spread about me on Facebook and I can't take it.
-When I was younger I was bullied. Now I am a bully. How can I help myself?
-I have been bullied so bad, and left out all my life. It's the worst on the bus and it's so bad that I think of killing myself.
-How can I get through being bullied? I have never fit in.
-What do I do when I'm being pushed around and ignored?
-Why doesn't anybody have any respect these days?
-Everyone labels and judges and I'm sick of it.
-I feel so bad when the popular kids bully the unpopular kids.
-How do I stand up to bullies and make them stop making me feel like garbage?

It hurts to realize that someone else would go to the trouble to try to make you feel so badly about yourself; perhaps even going so far as to say that you should not even exist. If you have been bullied, disrespected, belittled or outcast remember: you are the child of the Creator of the universe and *no one can ever take that away from you.* Decide that you will accept responsibility for your feelings and never again allow another person to make you feel bad about who you are.

Please let go of any thoughts of taking your life. It can certainly hurt to feel that others look down upon you. Decide right now: ***that you will never again allow another human being determine how you are going to feel about yourself.***

WHY? Because if someone has felt the need to make themselves feel strong by making you look or feel weak; *they are the one with the problem not you.* It is a cheap and immature tactic that reveals that they themselves do not love their life. They do not like the way they are inside. This is a fact, because when someone loves their life, they never even get the thought that they should try to make someone else feel like they should not love theirs. When you love the way you shine, don't have two seconds to waste trying to make someone feel like they should not love the way they shine.

The younger generation did not invent bullying, but it is true that you are living in a society with an increased tolerance for cruelty and character assassination. You also have the internet where it is possible to say things about others that are incredibly hurtful, without having to look them in the face. The additional cruelty about tormenting on the internet is that it feels like you are being put down in front of the whole world.
-*Someone on the internet told me I should kill myself, and it has been haunting me.*

That is a very upsetting thing to go through. Don't allow that evil act to haunt you. Ask God to help you move ahead, and not dwell on it. Stay away from any social media where people can post hateful messages anonymously.
-*How do I deal with a teacher who is cruel to me? Guidance does nothing.*

Confront them about it. If you get nowhere, or they take it out on you- let your parents or school administrator know.
-*I was bullied in second grade and again in middle school and now afraid for high school.*
"Yesterday does not equal tomorrow". It's a new beginning and the chances are most of them have grown up a little, and will not enjoy it as much. Besides- don't let them get a reaction out of you. Bullying is no fun if they can't make you upset.

Burying Feelings

-*How can I learn to show my emotions more?*
-*I beat myself up for not crying at my cousin's funeral.*

-I am always burying and hiding my emotional pain. What can I do?
　　The habit of holding in emotions usually starts following an experience of feeling vulnerable. The brain, which functions like a computer, has the job of protecting you from harm. Once you have been hurt, it will attempt to protect you from further pain. It will encourage you to build a wall of protection around yourself; never let anybody in, and never reveal anything that could cause you any further pain. Sometimes it is good to listen to the brain; sometimes not. Remember that you are the one who is supposed to run the brain as opposed to the brain running you. The brain is supposed to serve your soul, not be automatically controlled by it. There is a tremendous freedom that comes with this realization, and living according to it. To know that you have that ability to choose. If you live life automatically following whatever the brain says, you will end up doing nothing, since the brain will always cast everything in the light of being too risky and dangerous. It is no life at all, since emotions are a powerhouse of energy for life. Ask God's Holy Spirit for the courage to live fully alive; knowing that whatever hurts life and others may throw at you, you will survive.

Conflict/Drama
-What do you do if you apologized and they won't forgive you?
-Why do people crush other people's dreams?
-How do you know what is the right thing to do when
　　something makes you happy but not other people?
There is way too much drama in my school. I'm getting sick of it.
　　Conflict is a natural part of life. You will always be in situations where people do not act the way you would, or believe as you do. You want to ask God's spirit to guide you through these situations.

Be a peacemaker. Be the one who reaches out to solve a conflict. It takes two people to make peace; and for reconciliation to happen. No matter how the other person responds, you will always know you tried.

Nothing is unforgivable; but there are some things that you have a right to say you will not allow in your life.

Pray and ask God's guidance. Pray that His will be done, not yours. Be willing to say to God that you are ready to do whatever he tells you is the right thing to do. This is how you will know what to tolerate, or not. It is how you will know whether to give someone a second or third chance.

Some people have many conflicts because they deep down are *really* angry about something *else*; and it comes out in everyday conflicts and resentments.

Regarding drama, there are people who actually enjoy it. They feel it adds something special to their life, and create as much of it as they can. Life presents plenty of its own dram, creating more and hyping things up more is totally ridiculous. if you agree, then simply refuse to get caught up in it. Leave that group if necessary, and if the drama ever becomes about you, never make it your problem. It's theirs.

-Is it possible to support as person while not agreeing with what they do?

Yes, but it can be very challenging. In cases of close relationships, it is crucial to maintaining the love.

<u>Dealing with conflict:</u>
1-Try to understand the other persons experience, feelings and thoughts about the situation; then you will be able to speak with them in a way they will understand.
2-Stick with the facts as you feel about them, and never resort to name-calling. It never helps, and neither does accusing or

cruel criticizing. It forces them to stick up for themselves and crates drama rather than solving the conflict.
3-Remember that your goal is to bring out the truth, and not to reject or even to win the argument. The preservation of the relationship while maintaining honesty is your real goal
4-Perhaps practice what you wish to say with someone else in advance. It can help you anticipate their responses and see solutions more clearly.
5-Above all strive for the truth and a solution, not victory. It doesn't help you if you've won the argument, but nothing has been solved, and/or a relationship has been shattered.

Cutting/ self harm
-I cut myself. I am starting to cut my thighs so no one will see.
-I am depressed and cut myself. I hide it from everyone.
-I cut myself and pull out my eyelashes due to anxiety because I'm bullied. I don't know how to stop.
-I am cutting myself, smoking weed & drinking to cover up my pain
-I cut and burn myself and can't stop. I went through a horrible trauma and believe it's all my fault and I deserve the pain and I can't turn to anybody
-My friend is cutting.

Self-harming is a serious concern. It is estimated that 40% of American teens are involved. Stopping this habit can be very challenging, and requires the assistance of professional help, a counselor that has the specific skills to help you or a friend rewire the brain, so that what is obtained through cutting, burning or other self-harming can be attained in a much healthier manner. It is more that just working through poor self-esteem. Make sure you or a friend is in the care of someone who knows this.
How you can help a friend or loved one who is cutting:

-Don't demand that they stop instantly- you can't MAKE someone stop doing this.
-Express your love, concern and confidence in them. It will help move them into getting help.
-Try to understand what they've been through and how difficult it will be to stop.
-Don't overreact or appear shocked, anxious or frightened.
-Remember: cutting is not usually an attempt at suicide or a way to get attention; but is an outward sign of emotional distress.
-Don't overreact, but also don't ignore .
-Be patient; it takes time for confidence to grow.
-Never say to a cutter: "You are really messed up." This is a condemning comment, and for someone who already feels out of control, it reinforces feelings of powerlessness. It makes the cutter feel more shame. Their self-mutilation is not about you; don't inject your personal feelings into it.
-Loyalty over a period of time speaks louder than words.
-Pray for them.

Death
-*There have been numerous deaths in my life.*
-*My mother has had three miscarriages.*
-*My baby brother died at 5 months old. Why?*
-*My mother passed away when I was little. I watched it happen and I couldn't do anything to help her. I need to forgive myself.*
-*My dad died and I try to talk to my friends, but no one really understands.*
-*My grandpa died and he was my best friend.*

Dealing with death is one of the greatest challenges that we can face in this life. It gives me no joy to say this, but it is true and important to realize "that everyone you will ever love will die." It is the nature of life on the physical level that no one lives forever in their body. So it is important not to waste tremendous energy and agony asking "why did they have to die?"

The death of a loved one is something that comes into every life; and when it does your prayer is "for the peace and healing to accept the loss." It also helps to remember what our faith teaches: that the dead do not cease to exist and that we will see them again. Science now backs this up. Science says that energy cannot be destroyed; it can only change form.

What is particularly painful is the loss of a child or a young person. In the natural scheme of things it seems so unjust that their earthly life should be cut short.

Allow yourself to grieve. Healing takes time; sometimes in cases of a significant loss, as much as a year or two before you feel like yourself again. Longer than this, professional help may be be beneficial. The goal is not to get to the point where you no longer miss the person. It's not about getting over it; it's getting through it and finding a way to hold the loved one in your heart as you move forward. The only thing worse than feeling sad because someone has died, is to feel nothing; because that would mean there was no love there. The sadness means there was something special you shared; and that kind of love never dies.

-My brother died, how do I move on? I never got to say goodbye.
Some people get the gift of being able to be with someone right before or when they die; and an awful lot do not. Take comfort that the person who had died, now exists in a larger reality and knows how you feel about them. If they were a person who loved God and others, you can know that they are praying for you. If they were not, or you really don't know for sure, then pray for them to find peace and healing in the afterlife.

-Death is my biggest fear. Am I going to be remembered?
Facing your own death can be one of the greatest aides to living your life to the fullest. Remember that we don't die. We simply do not live forever in these bodies.
Wondering how you will be remembered can propel you to living a love-centered life like nothing else.

Depression/Anxiety

-I have severe anxiety, and I can't say anything because I know my family doesn't have the money for counseling
-I'm depressed and I don't want to tell my parents because they may think less of me.
-My mother won't let me talk about my depression, and says I just like sulking. I know it's not just that and I feel unloved.
-My friend is very depressed and nothing I do or say helps.
-My sister is depressed & dropped out of college.
-I can't sleep.
-I am depressed and I don't know why or how to get through it.
-What should you do when you feel depressed?
-How do you help a person who tries to be happy, but has so many bad things happen to them?
-My grandpa is always depressed and I can never make him smile, and he makes everyone else depressed too.
-My father's drinking and verbal abuse has caused my mother to go into a depression.
-Even though I know God loves me and I have family and friends who love me, I cannot stop crying myself to sleep at night.

Depression and anxiety are nothing to be ashamed of. They happen to many people.

Depression feels like a deep, dark hole you can't escape from. Everyone has times when they feel down; depression is more than that. A depressed person shows or experiences a variety of symptoms: sadness, tearfulness, fatigue, poor concentration, insomnia, over-sleeping, loss of appetite, over-eating, loss of interest in things they previously enjoyed, irritability, anger, agitation, lethargy, suicidal thoughts, cutting or self-harming, or feelings of guilt, hopelessness, or worthlessness for more than just a few days.

Depression can occur when personal stress and pain becomes too much. The United Nations says that at least 1/3 of the human race is in deep depression. Everyone experiences depression at some time in their life. If it has gotten out of control, and persists for you or someone you care about for a long time, then get professional help.

-*I am always anxious about doing something because of what other people might think.*

Don't do this. it doesn't help. Remember that no one is perfect and has things about themselves they don't like. Do what you have to do anyway. Things usually get easier with practice.

-*I get anxious about upsetting situations.*

First think about whether you you seeing the situation clearly or not. Try and see another person's point of view to see how they might feel in the same situation. Talk things out with a good friend, and/or trusted adult. Do something physical, relaxing or to help someone else. Stepping away for a bit helps shift your perspective.

Anxiety is an unpleasant state of inner turmoil; a feeling of dread over something unlikely to happen, which might be accompanied by nervous behavior like pacing, restlessness, fatigue, or difficulty in concentrating. Anxiety is not the same as fear, which is felt about something realistically intimidating or dangerous, and is an appropriate response to a perceived threat.

When anxiety becomes overwhelming and distressing to the sufferer, it may require professional help.

Always have Jesus in your heart with you when you go to a counselor, asking Him to guide you through the session together.

Important: Go to a counselor first, not a psychiatrist.

Many psychiatrists today will readily prescribe an antidepressant or two, without even listening to you talk about what you are going through. Avoid these, and seek someone who cares and will listen before prescribing medication.

If you are afraid of being judged by your family, don't let that fear stop you. It's a natural fear, but remember if they love you, they will not think less of you, and will do everything they can to help. If your family lacks the money to pay for counseling your local church probably has resources and connection available for you.

If you are a teenager, and it's your friend who is depressed or severely anxious, continue to listen to and support them as a friend, but remember treating this is over your head. It is OK and important to recognize that at your age you do not have to have all the answers. Get them to professional help, or someone who can help them and their family arrange that.

If it's a family member, speak with other adults in the family who may be able to do more. No matter what: most definitely pray for yourself, and/ or the depressed person.

Divorce

-Out of nowhere my father says he doesn't love my mother anymore and is leaving. Now they hate each other.
-My divorcing parents are putting so much pressure on me to decide to live with each of them. I am so scared of not pleasing either and I will lose one or both of them.
-My parents divorce is my fault.
-My parents split & I get bounced between them like a ping-pong ball.

-My parents are divorcing and I feel as though it is my fault
-My parents are divorced & my mom is always trying to make me not love my dad, and it's breaking apart our relationship.
-My parents and most of my relatives are divorced or miserable.   Is real love even possible these days?
-My father's new wife is cruel to me and he takes her side.
-My mother cares more for her new boyfriend than me.

Half of all marriages end in divorce, and while most parents would never want their children to get hurt by their divorce, most do.

There are countless ways in which the divorce can affect a young person and present many challenges.

Some are blamed by the parents for their unhappiness, or blame themselves for the divorce. It is never the child's fault that the parents split or divorce. It's natural, especially for small children, to relate to everything emotionally and take everything personally. It's important to remember: parents are responsible for their relationship and marriage is incredibly difficult. Children often feel "I was supposed to make them happy" or "if I would have been a perfect enough child, they would have worked this out for me" or "if I could have made them laugh one more time, maybe they could have tried one more time to get along."

It doesn't go like that. It was not your job to make them happy, or make their marriage successful. Let go of that burden right now. I have met young people for whom it didn't matter how well they did at their school work or sports or anything. They felt that they were a failure because they had judged that what really mattered, keeping their family together, they had failed at. Let that go.

Other young people have lived in a beautiful house; and nobody was ever happy in it. Some grow up living in a war zone; coming to believe that the world is not a good place because throughout their young lives they were frightened. They had to watch the two people, who were supposed to be taking care of them hurt each other.

Some have parents who don't know when to shut their mouths. They put the children in the middle "Tell you mother this," "Tell your father that," "Don't tell your mother this," etc. Some parents become bent on poisoning their child against the other parent.

Some really love holidays, summer vacation and birthdays because with divorced parents they will often fall all over each other trying to out-do the other parent with what they'll buy or do for you so you'll love them more than the other one. Meanwhile, what you really would have liked was to have lived in a home where people were happy and loved each other. You may have been given everything, but you didn't get that.

Some lose a parent from the divorce. One of them leaves, and makes another family, and it becomes very clear that that's what they really care about now. Maybe they even treat you like you're part of some big mistake they made.

Some are treated badly by the mother's new husband or boyfriend; or the father's new wife or girlfriend. Sometimes worse than that, that person is disrespectful or abusive to you, and your parent sticks up for them instead of you, because they are afraid of losing them.

Some have to wonder all the rest of their lives if both their parents be there for their big life events, and if they do both attend, will they be respectful or create a scene.

Remember:
1- Parents unhappiness and splitting is primarily their issue, not yours.
2- Your parents misery, or not being able to continue to live together, does not now mean that you were an accident.

3- If they made their promise to each other on an altar before God, they owe it to God, each other, and you to go for marriage counseling before they make any decision to split. If they do not, then they cannot assure anybody that they have done every possible thing to save their marriage. The marriage counselor will be a neutral person who will allow both side to speak their mind, and make sure they are heard, and help them not only see their issues, but come up with possible solutions.

4- Pray for your parents and for yourself.

5- You have a right to stick up for yourself if they attempt to put you in the middle, or poison you against the other. Don't let one parent put down the other in front of you. Remind them that you don't have to hate one to love the other; it's THEIR divorce, not YOURS. Tell both your parents that you want to see them, often.

6- Forgive them for any and all ways you have been hurt by their divorce.

7- Express your feelings if one of your parents starts to fall out of your life, or has a negative or even abusive partner. Let them know if you experience being pushed aside in favor of siblings born through the new union. Be specific in pointing out why you feel the way you do. it may or may not change anything; but you'll always know you tied to communicate and stick up for yourself.

8- Focus on your own life, not theirs. Keep busy

If your parents remarry:

1-let your parent spend time with your stepparent, and don;t force them to choose between them and you.

2-If you feel left out, speak up and work out a compromise

3-Do something loving for your stepparent

Is real love possible in this selfish world? YES! While it may be rare, it *is* possible and worth it, and worth waiting for. Remember: you will never be happy in a relationship with a person who only knows how to think of, and take care of themselves. Don't wait to be a giving and loving person. Then when you meet someone you can make a good life with because they also are able to commit to love, you will be ready.

Drugs
-I am worried about my friend on drugs. He won't recognize that he has a problem.
-Someone I care about is doing very serious drugs, and I am afraid of losing them.
-How do I make my older brother stop doing drugs? No one in the family wants to deal with it. My money and my stuff are always missing, and I know he's stealing it for drugs.
-My father is addicted to drugs and he always forgets my birthday.
-My mother is doing drugs and leaving the house for the last 2 years. I am hurt and angry with her.
-My mom does drugs. She tries to hide it and doesn't think I know.
-My moms brother did heroin, and it tore the family apart. We don't see her side of the family anymore.
-How do you get over watching your brother kill himself with drugs and not caring about anyone but himself?
-My cousin does drugs & went to jail. What made her do this?
-My brother is addicted to drugs and I don't want to lose him. Since drugs took over his life my family has never been the same.
-I am addicted to drugs.
-I'm addicted to weed. I can't go a day without lighting up.
-What's the big deal with smoking weed? It's legal in some places.

Drugs, both legal and illegal, are everywhere. For some people, drugs will be a distraction from life, or from pain. For others, with addictive personalities, or who get into hardcore drugs, they become a means of self-destruction.

Regardless if it is a parent, friend, sibling or other relative who is addicted to drugs, legal or illegal, read the Alcohol section. Since alcohol is a drug, the ways to deal with other drugs are the same.

Regarding marijuana:
Many are confused now since it is illegal in some places and not others, and some wonder "how bad can it be if you can take it if you have a medical condition?"
There are still reasons to be concerned with marijuana:
1- It is still a doorway to other drugs
2- While it may not be physically addictive, it can be
    psychologically addictive for some
3- It often leads to lethargy, especially in the young
4- The research has consistently shown that it is especially damaging to the young, negatively affecting the development of teens brains
5- It still affects judgment. People do a lot of things under the influence of weed; like any other drug, that they might not do otherwise, often making poor, and even disastrous decisions regarding sex, crime, driving, and risky actions.
6- DUI (driving under the influence) is a serious crime.
7- Where smoking, distributing and possession of marijuana is illegal, the moral thing to do is to obey the law.

Altered states of reality will always be tempting. The key is to live in reality without needing or wanting a substance to get you through it or take you out of it. ***The best thing is to strive for is a drug free life.*** Once you have your body, mind, soul, and emotions fully alive and in harmony; the need for any substance that will give you the artificial illusion of that well-being goes away.

Eating Disorders

-I feel fat, people have always made fun of my weight and now I have an eating disorder.
-My cousin has been tormented by people. Now she does drugs and won't eat and her hair is starting to fall out. She comes to me for advice and I don't know what to do.
- I'm uncomfortable with my weight and barely eat, starving myself.

Eating disorders are a serious situation today. Statistics say that 1 in 100 teens has anorexia, or bulimia. Eating disorder challenges are connected to body image. *(Read that section.)* If it's you or someone you care about, know that an intense program of treatment may be needed. Don't ignore the signs; get help. Prayer is important, as is remembering that God loves you, no matter what; but get help! Make sure the counselor you go to specifically knows how to help someone with an eating disorder *(not everyone does).*

Emotional Pain

-My heart is overflowing with emotion. I cry everyday.
-How do you get over feelings you don't want to have and have been holding onto for too long?

Feeling strong emotions are a natural part of life, but when they become overwhelming, for prolonged periods of time, or are not proportionate to reality, it's time to get professional help.

-I wish I could take on the illnesses of my family members because I hate knowing I am happy and they have to go through this.

God bless you for having the good heart for wanting to do this, but the best way you can help those you love who are suffering is to be with them, assist them if needed, and pray for them. Radiate your happiness for them, don't wish it away.

-How can I let my emotions out to my friends instead of keeping everything bottled up?

Pain is part of life, and so are emotions. They are neither good nor bad. What we do with them can be good or bad. Becoming stuck emotionally can easily happen; and sometimes it can take a while to figure out why you are overly emotional or emotionally dead. When this happens it is completely normal to speak with someone about it. Start with someone you trust and then a professional person if necessary, especially if it's too intense.
-I tried talking to a counselor once and it didn't help.
No one understands me.
First really take a look at yourself. You could have the best counselor in the world, but if you are not ready to make use of the session, you will experience no growth. Maybe it's you who was resistant. Maybe you didn't give it enough time. Their job is not to give you the answers. A good counselor will know what questions to ask you to help you figure out the answers for yourself.
Counseling is like any other profession; there's good and there's bad. If it was the counselor, don't give up on counseling; try another counselor.

Failure

-I am not a good student and always disappointing everyone.
-I dropped a pass that made us lose a championship, and now everyone hates me.
-Will my future be as successful as I want it to be?
-I am having so much trouble passing and doing well in school compared to everyone else. I really try but it's not good enough.

Everybody has the experience of things not turning out the way they would have liked. You could label them failures. Or you can consider them learning experiences; and that will make all the difference.
Parents, coaches, and caring adults have a responsibility to challenge you to do the best you can in life. If you are not as good a

student as others in your family, or being told you're a disappointment, ask yourself honestly: are you really trying to do the best you can? If you know you are really giving it your best, then you have integrity inside no matter what anyone else says.

You might choke in a big pressure situation, and fear that everyone will label you a loser all your life. The bottom line is: you can't control what people are going to say and the only labels that matter are the ones that you and God hold to. Even though you are growing, and becoming better every day, God loves and accepts the person you are at any given time. You may come up short, you may sin; but your ultimate identity is not loser or sinner. You are a human being, a child of the Creator of the universe, made purposely and lovingly. No setback and nobody can take that away from you.

> *"This is just a small setback on the way to a big comeback."*
> Young man @ the Juvenile Detention Center

In baseball a hitter that gets a lifetime annual .333 batting average will be in the Hall of Fame. That batting average means that they made out 2/3 of the time. 2/3 of the time they did not get a hit; and yet they are among the best. Allow what others would call a failure to be for you a learning experience.

> PS: a game is never lost by just one player or one play, and true athletes know that.

-Is it possible to move on after a really bad mistake?
Yes; but you may have to pay a price for it. In some cases it may take some time to regain the trust of others.

Family Challenges
-There is a family feud going on and my family is breaking apart.

-Before the family feud we used to have so much fun together and now we don't even see each other. I know they don't do it to hurt us kids, but we cousins used to be so close.
-My aunt and uncle divorced, and I'm afraid I won't see my cousins again.
-My cousin treats everything like a joke.
-A family member is not able to have a baby what should they do?
-I have a bipolar family member.
-My grandpa acts like a jerk. He torments my father and never comes to any of my events.
-My uncle has separated himself from our family and it's breaking my mother's heart.
-My family overreacts and fights about everything, and I'm afraid it will never be fixed.

    There will always be challenges with people in life and none are probably more painful than the ones we have to go through with our families. Some things we may be saddened or even horrified by; but ultimately not able to do anything about: divorces, imprisonment, the inability to have children, a mental condition, etc. Pray for those family members, especially if they are going through it without faith.

    Sometimes we have to have the courage to take action. If there is a family feud, talk with your parents about how upset and disappointed you are. Search for someone who could be a peacemaker. Let your grandpa know how you miss him and wish he could be a bigger part of your life. Let your cousin know how you felt when he didn't take something serious that was important. Let your cousins know that even though their parents are divorced, you still care about them and want to stay close to them. All these things may not work out the way you want, but they are worth fighting for and no matter what, you'll always know you tried.

-My family will not support my dreams.
Let them know how this affects you; but no matter what they do or say, ask Jesus to show you the way, and give you the strength to follow the path to travel with Him.

How are you supposed to help a family member that is much older than you?
It can be challenging; but you have to try. No one likes being corrected or challenged by someone younger. Most people believe they are supposed to know better; and when it is revealed that the younger person is right, they become embarrassed. Pray for a way for them to make a change that is not so threatening; and if you speak out to them yourself- be respectful: clear, but kind.

Friendship Challenges
-My friends just use me. They say they want to be friends, but I know I'm just going to get hurt.
-My friend always hurts me; but I don't want to lose the friendship.
-How can I keep a friendship from dying?
-My friends are bad influences.
-My childhood friend and I have grown very far apart. I knew her my whole life and now it seems like we don't even know each other.
-A really good friend changed for the worse when she got to high school. I want to help her, but she never talks with me anymore.
-People I consider my friend have been saying many cruel things about me.

Fight to hold onto your friendships that you would like to keep; but remember- it takes two to make it work. Understand that very few friendships are for an entire lifetime. Those are rare, so if you have one- treasure it. Most friendships are for a particular time in life: elementary school, a sports team, a club, middle school, high school, college, workplace, living in a particular neighborhood. It's a natural thing that some friendships will end when one or both friends have moved on. Some people develop new interests, have conflicts, change schools or jobs, move, become different people from the way they were, or develop bad habits. All kinds of things can lead to friendships ending and people going in different directions.

If you are having a conflict or difficulty with a friend, speak with them. Do it calmly, without laying a guilt trip on them. Reach out to a friend who has grown distant. Tell them what the friendship means to you, and how you feel about it slipping away.
One of three things will happen:
1- "You're right. We have grown apart, and that's because I've moved on. have a great life." That will hurt; but at least you'll know.
2- "I'm sorry, let's make it work." They do better for awhile; but then they go back to leaving you out of their life.
3- "I'm so glad you brought it up. I noticed it too, and I don't want to lose you either." and you have a friend maybe for life.
No matter what happens, you know you had the guts to fight for it.
-I need to make new friends. How do I do that?
Get involved in activities that you enjoy. There you will find people who have things in common with you. Also get involved in activities where people bond by doing something intense together like: sports, plays, retreats, service projects, mission trips.
-My friends are pressuring me to drug and do drugs.
Let your friends know that you not into it. Telling them individually is easier than taking on a crowd. True friends will respect your decision, and you may even give them the courage to resist those things too. State your feelings in a way that does not make them feel like they are being put down. Some might give you a hard time, so pray for the strength to stick to your convictions.

Friends with challenges
-I don't know how to stop my friend from doing bad things.
-My friend is hanging out with the wrong people and making bad decisions
-My friend is part of the Illuminati- how do I change him?

When someone you care about is going down the wrong path you have to say something, or get someone in a better position to say something. Sometimes people don't say anything when a friend is making bad choices because they are pretty sure they'll deny that there is an issue and they're afraid they will turn on them, and end the friendship. Think of your biggest nightmare: something catastrophic happens to a friend as a result of the bad stuff they were into. You knew it was wrong, but you never said anything. Are you going to be able to sleep at night? No. So that's the sign that you need to do something.

When you open your mouth, one of these things will happen:

1- They will ignore you or unload their anger on you, get defensive and try to make you feel foolish for bringing it up

2- They may do better for awhile; but never really change or get the help they may need to really change, and then slip back into their bad habit

3- They may hear the loving voice of God speaking through you and go for it. Sometimes people are really crying out for help by what they are doing, and just need to hear that someone else cares enough to see and say something.

No matter what they do, you know you tried.

Nobody changes anything until they're ready.

The most important thing you can do is pray for them. All the good we wish for for someone happens first on the spiritual level. You may not be the immediate reason for them changing, but through prayer you will always be part of their healing. If they don't listen to you, pray that someone else will come into their life that they might listen to. Often people don't want to be told that they are messing up by the people closest to them.

-My friend is going through a hard time, but won't let me help them.
-My friend won't share her emotions & tell me what's troubling her
It's very painful to see someone you care about hurting and they won't let you be there for them. Stay close, let them know they can come to you anytime, and you'll be happy to be there for them. Don't take it personally. People don't open up until, if, and when they're ready.

Gangs
-My friend was killed from gang violence.
-My boys got my back. They're the only ones I can trust;
    but I keep getting into trouble with them.
-How do I resist joining a gang?
You MUST resist joining a gang. It's so much easier not to ever get into that world in the first place, than to have to leave it. Pray to be spiritually strong. Know that God is the only strength you need. Show respect for your friends in the gang, but then strongly, yet politely, refuse to join.

The temptation to join a group that will have your back can be very great. More than half of the young people I work with in jail every week are in some gang. Most live in communities where there is a lot of danger, and gangs give the appearance of security. Also most young people have a desire to belong to something bigger than themselves, and gangs provide that too. The camaraderie gives the sense that these are the people you can count on when you will need them.

The difficulty comes in when dangerous, criminal and violent activities are involved. I have told countless young people in gangs in prison that those gang members are not their real friends. They usually respond "*They got my back*". I ask them "*Where are they now?*" I tell them "Maybe they do have your back, but have you ever thought about how they get you into so many situations where you *need* them to have your back". I tell them "In life your friends don't lead you into trouble. Your **real** friends lead you **away** from trouble. Real friends challenge you to be the **best** person you can be, **not** the worst."

If you are already in a gang, it can be very difficult to get out, painful but possible, if you do it the right way without showing disrespect.

Guilt & Shame
-I feel guilty for being so happy when people I know, and people everywhere are suffering.

While it is good that you feel for those who are suffering, refusing to be joyful in the midst of that does not help them. There will always be people suffering. Hold them in your heart and honor them by spreading your joy. Pray for God to show you how He wants to work through, and with you, and the unique gifts and vision He gave you to help heal the suffering in the world with His love.

-I am filled with guilt. I hurt someone bad & they won't forgive me.
-I saw someone treated cruelly and I said nothing. I feel responsible now and mad at myself for not saying something.

Remember that guilt is not a bad thing. It is your conscience letting you know that you have not done what's right, and gone against your moral code. Thank God you have Jesus in your heart, and now feel compassion for that person who got hurt.
God forgives you, so forgive yourself, learn from the experience and move on. Pray for that person you neglected to help and if there is a way for you to make it up to or right with them.

Hopelessness
-Why do bad things always get worse? There's no hope.
-Can horrible situations get better? I just want everything to be OK.
-I got used, I don't believe in love anymore. I stopped caring.
-Is it possible to move on after a really bad mistake?
-Does hatred follow you or do you create it?
-I am afraid that I will never be myself again.

    Hopelessness is a pattern of thinking, where you believe that the misery you are trapped in will never go away, and things will never get better. It's easy to sink into, but don't give into it. Avoid the temptation to lose hope, and do nothing. Depression and hopelessness kick in when we are unable to do something about things that are seriously affecting us. It is important here to remember *the serenity prayer (page 12)*. You may be frustrated simply from trying to change something that you ultimately should accept. You might be overwhelmed by trying to change something that you are simply not in a position to completely remedy. In these cases, do what you can, and put the rest in God's hands. Change and new beginnings are possible. Sometimes things get worse before they get better. Continue to have faith in love.

> ***Yesterday does not equal tomorrow***

Jealousy
-I find I am jealous and hateful of many people. I wish I had their life instead of mine.
-Other girls are so cruel to me. I think they are jealous of me.
-I have not yet figured out what I'm good at and I am jealous of others.

    People become jealous of each other when they have self doubts, and when they believe that they are in competition with the person they are jealous of. Pray to learn how to accept yourself.

Some tips:
- Build your self-confidence.
- Fix your mental and physical image of yourself.
- Deal with feelings of insecurity.
- Conquer your fears, whether it's a fear of abandonment or fear of rejection.
- Do some external changes; fix your mistakes.
- Be assertive; communicate your feelings without being aggressive nor allowing your rights to be violated.
- Control your anger; a direct result of jealousy that will also destroy your relations with others.

Loneliness/ Isolation/Withdrawal
- *How can you make someone feel that they are not alone?*
- *I cry myself to sleep at night worrying that I am not good enough for anyone. Everyone I love leaves.*
- *I feel unimportant and left out. Everyone has something they are good at except me.*
- *People treat me like I'm invisible.*
- *I feel so left out in my family, and spend all my time at home alone.*
- *I am constantly losing friends & don't have anyone to talk to anymore.*
- *I've been bullied and left out all my life.*
- *I'm isolated from my family.*
- *I feel left out- so I push everyone away.*
- *I am a floater. I don't belong in any particular clique or group.*
- *How can I stop feeling alone?*
- *My crush rejected me and I feel like I will never be loved.*
- *I am afraid that I can't be myself anymore and I am never going to fit in.*
- *I have been alone for so long that I'm afraid my heart has gone dark and even dead.*

-I want someone who appreciates me for who and how I am, but I'm so scared of what they'll do to me.
-When I'm upset I can't talk with anyone because I don't want them to judge me.
-How do I let myself trust others and not be so closed off to everyone?
-I am always feeling lonely.
-How do you handle rejection?
There is a difference between feeling lonely and alone.

Sometimes when it feels like no one loves us, or no one is close to us, it's really one specific person who we want to like us and be with that we are missing. In life sometimes you can have such strong feelings toward someone that when they don't feel the same way, or even feel an opposite way, it seems so wrong. "How can it be that I could feel so much, and they don't even want to be close to me?"

Loneliness is a feeling of emptiness or hollowness inside you. You feel isolated or separated from the world, cut off from those you would like to have contact with, and sad about it. There are different kinds of loneliness, and different degrees of loneliness. It could be a vague feeling that something is not right, a kind of minor emptiness. Or a very intense, deep pain. It might be related to missing a specific individual because they have died or because they are so far away. It might involve feeling alone and out of contact with people because you are actually physically isolated from people. You might even feel emotionally isolated when you are surrounded by people, but are having trouble reaching out to them.

Loneliness is a passive state that can be changed:
-Recognize, admit and express the lonely feelings.
-Become more active.
-Get involved in activities or clubs.

-Never clutch and grab at people and experiences to avoid loneliness. There are times and places in this life where it is better to be alone that to be in with the wrong people.
-Remember and strengthen your God connection. The truth is that we are never alone. Our Creator is closer to us than we are to ourselves so when you have God in your life you are never alone.

Money Challenges

-My parents don't have the money to send me to college.
-I am always afraid my family will run out of money.
-I am very scared that because of my brother's medical bills, my parents won't be able to afford my tuition.
-My family is having financial problems. Our home is in foreclosure.

Struggling financially when you are in a poor country is rough, but at least you know you're not alone. Struggling in a place where many or most people are doing very well is far worse because you feel like a failure compared to everyone around you.
You can make a difference in your family when financial challenges hit:
1- Cut down your own spending- use the experience to focus on what matters, which is people, and not things. look for inexpensive and free ways to have fun.
2- Find ways to help. Get a job and make something to help pay the family bills. Maybe have a yard sale, sell stuff to your friends or on Amazon or E-Bay.
3-Pray for your parent who may be out of work, that they find a job and have some peace in the meantime. It can be very demoralizing (especially for fathers) to feel that they are unable to support their families.
4- Remember that you and your family have God, life, and each other and this is more important than anything.

Moving

-My sister is away at college and I miss her; but she doesn't seem to miss me.
-My brother is in the military now, and I am so scared something bad will happen to him and I miss him so much.
-I am moving, and I'm afraid of losing all my friends.
-My family member had to move far away to get a job.

  People who are close to you moving away because of their job or military is the kind of thing that you cannot change. What you *can* do is make every effort to stay close by keeping in contact. With family and friends, fight to keep the connection alive. If it becomes one-sided, then let them know how you feel. If nothing changes, then accept that perhaps they have moved on, and ask God to heal the pain of that loss, accepting that while some friendships are for forever, some friendships are only for a period in our lives.

  When someone you love is in the military, you can keep in regular contact with them. Hearing from loved ones is something they enjoy very much. Make sure to pray for them regularly; especially if they have no faith. Serving in war conditions without faith can be unbearable. Also remember to pray for loved ones who have returned from war; their scars and deepest wounds may be unseen.

Parent conflicts & challenges

-How do you deal with a parent who never sees the good in you?
-My parents are always fighting and I am afraid they'll divorce and they always trace it back to me.
-My parents are always fighting and I always end up in the middle. The only time they get along is when they're drunk.
-My parents blame me for their fighting.
-How can I have a better relationship with my dad if he walked out on me and all of us and won't communicate?

-My mom is dating someone 16 years younger than she is.
-My parents love my brother more than me- I am always being compared & considered the disappointment of the family.
-How do I talk about it to a parent who does not approve of my relationship?
-I found out that my parents have been lying to me about something bad that happened in the family. Now I don't know how many other things they are lying to me about or keeping from me.
-My mom doesn't care about me as much as my baby siblings.
-My father has never said he is proud of me or that he loves me. I feel worthless & unloved.
-My mother is never satisfied with my grades. I feel like I am never good enough.
-My father has said I never should have been born.
-My parents don't appreciate anything I do. They are never proud of me.
-My parents force me to live up to their expectations.
-My mother is always comparing me to my friend.
-My father never keeps his word on what he says he will do. What can I do?
-What do you do when you feel your father doesn't love you?
-My father cannot take anyone showing any feelings.
-My parents live in the same house, but never speak.
-My mother had an abortion and I am so angry and ashamed.
-My mother is so cruel. She belittles me constantly and beats me over nothing.
-There is a lot of favoritism with my parents & I am the least favorite.
-My parents and siblings are fighting. They won't listen when I tell them to compromise. What next?
-My parents are always fighting about money and drinking.
-I wish I had a real mother/daughter relationship.

-Is it bad to tell your parents to get a divorce because they are fighting all the time?
-My father has anger issues. He thinks it is OK to take his anger out on me in violence.
-I don't know what to do about my emotionally abusive dad.
-My parents love my brother more than me- I am always being compared and considered the disappointment of the family.
-I can't forgive my father for what he has put my family through.
-My dad has been horribly violent with my mom. I was too young to do anything about it. He doesn't act like a dad and I would like him to.
-How do I love a parent who has abandoned me?

Obviously this is one of the biggest areas of challenge for young people. The people that God gives to us as parents are probably the two most important people in most of our lives, and so when conflicts and human weakness flare up, it can also be the most painful.

Nobody has perfect parents, because nobody is perfect. They are doing the best they can; but when their actions hurt you:
when they say cruel things, favor a sibling, fail to affirm or support you, are overly critical, pressure you excessively, are fighting with each other, hurt and betray:

Communicate. Sometimes adults are not aware of the impact of their actions on their children. If you are being hurt by something they are doing to you, a sibling or each other, let them know.

They may ignore you or turn on you. No parent wants to be corrected by their child. You may not get an apology or immediate change; but you could see change down the line.

Or they may change for a bit, but then go back to their ways, in which case you will have to speak to them again.

Or you have provided them with a wake-up call. They may give you a heartfelt apology or explanation, and real change in your relationship could begin immediately.
But you have to say something, otherwise you'll always wonder if it might have changed if you had said something.
****If violence is involved get outside help.

If you feel parents don't understand you, let them know how you feel, and force them to make time for you by making an appointment if necessary or write them a letter.
If your parents are overly critical, ask them for details, and let them know they have been heard. Keep them on your side by showing love and appreciation for them, and treat them the way you want to be treated. Talk with them about their lives as teenagers. it might help them remember what it feels like for you.

If your parents are overprotective, remember that they make their rules because they love you and don't want to see you get hurt. Show them you understand the dangers they are afraid of. If you can think of rules that would be more fair or appropriate for you, share them and ask your parents to give them a try.

Let your parents into your life. When they meet your friends and see who you are spending time with they will become more comfortable. There are a lot of unproductive things that teens say to their parents like "Everyone else is allowed to" "It's different these days". Your parents probably tried these same lines. They didn't work for them with their parents, and they won't work for you either.

If your parents fight, tell them how it bothers you (not during the argument of course). If necessary ask another family member to be a peacemaker. Try to understand both parents point of view, but don't take sides. While the fight is going on, take a break yourself, go for a walk, call a friend.

If your parents have issues with drugs and/or alcohol, don't let them blame you for their addiction. There is no way that it is your fault. If they have mood swings, it is their responsibility, not yours. So don't take things personally.
(Go to the "alcohol" section of this book for more information.)

Peer Pressure
-People expect so much from me and no one cares about how I feel.
-I have no real friends, they only hang around me to make themselves feel more beautiful. I am always at the bottom of the food chain.
-How do you deal with drama and peer pressure?
-I am tired of always having to change myself to fit in.
-My lunch table in school is a nightmare with people yelling and cursing and bullying.
-My friends want me to change. I don't think I'm doing anything wrong, but I don't want to lose them.
-I am not very social and do not have a lot of friends and scared to go into new situations.
-How do you stay strong when so much wrong is all around you?
-Online I was told anonymously to kill myself everyday.
-How do I get to be accepted?
-I'm socially awkward around others & don't fit in easily.
-When I am around others I feel like a needle in a haystack.

There is not much more important in life than maintaining your integrity. There is also a very strong need for each of us to belong. In life there is an ongoing struggle of balancing the two. Fitting in with and connecting with your peers is very important; and so is maintaining your moral code and your dignity.

If you find yourself in with a crowd that does not respect you stick up for yourself. Tell them that you need to see a change, and if it does not come, let them go. Don't ever be so desperate to belong or be accepted that you stay with people who don't respect you. They will feel justified in using you more and more; because you don't have the self- respect to stick up for yourself. Real friends never pressure you to break your moral code. They lead you away from trouble, not into trouble. Real friends bring out the best in you, challenging you to be the best person you can be, not the worst. Ask God for the strength to do the right thing, even if no one else cares to.

For some people it takes awhile to find the group where they really to fit in and belong- be patient, not desperate.

-Other kids are racist towards my friend. What should I do?
-Speak up for and defend your friend. Racism is an expression of small-mindedness and is wrong. You can't make them change, but you can offer them an opportunity to. No matter what, you have the integrity of knowing.

Physical challenges
-My cousin has autism and it is ruining my family.
-My little brother has autism and the family is suffering terribly.
-My brother was born with autism. People make fun of him in school and I feel so bad for him.

Autism is not the only challenge, but the number of people born with this condition is growing. Autism presents unique challenges to the autistic person, and to their families. Patience, love and respect are needed. Pray for that. If you have family members with this condition, be loving, make time for them.

Find ways to relieve the stress that parents go through. It is often helpful to join a support group for people who are struggling with the same challenge.

People born with disabilities (challenges is the correct term these days) do not want our sympathy. They want to be respected, loved and treated fully as human beings. Support them, include them and stick up for them if necessary.

Poor Self Image & Self Esteem/Insecurity

-I was told I was a mistake. I have negative self-esteem and have always believed I was useless and worthless.
-How can I ever live my dreams when no one in my own family believes in me?

No matter how anyone else has labeled your coming into the world based on their experience, you must remember that God meant for you to be here, and none of us who are in this life is an accident in HIS eyes. You are NOT the exception.

You must believe in yourself and the path God has made for you and Him to live out together even if no one else supports you. It is always painful when family, who are closest to us, don't support our decisions. usually they are fearful and trying to protect you. They deep down love you, so try to keep that in mind, but still follow your conscience.

-I am under so much pressure to be perfect and I am always under pressure.
-I may seem perfect, but I hate myself and I am so scared because no one notices.
-I am not good enough and have trouble accepting myself.
-I feel I have to be the best or else I will be worth nothing.
-Everyone is so judgmental.
-Why are people obsessed with perfection?

This is a very competitive society, and being number one is considered everything. All that matters is that you be the best YOU you can be. You will never be perfect, and that is OK. Strive to be the best you can; let God's perfection live in you, and leave the rest to Him.

-I have worn a mask all my life and now I don't know how to be who I really am.

Realizing and admitting you wear a mask if winning half the battle. Remember the futility of wearing a mask. if people like and accept you, there is no comfort, because they are relating to the front you present and not your real self. The next step is asking God to give you the courage to be your real self, no matter what the consequences. It might feel scary at times, but you will also experience incredible freedom. You will have incredibly more energy for life, because you will not be wasting any more energy maintaining a false identity.

-What do you do if you feel like you're worthless and mean nothing in life, you will never achieve and aren't good enough for anyone?
-I have trouble believing in myself & fear I have nothing to live for.
-How do I change how I see myself?
-How do I forgive myself after what I've done?
-I never feel like I am good enough, and I am always doing something wrong. I hate and doubt myself.
-How do I forget about people making fun of me?
-I was fat in middle school and had no friends and was always ditched at recess.
-I was bullied and now I worry way too much about how I look.
-I was made fun of everyday when I was younger & those memories still haunt me and I cannot believe in myself.

It's hard to forget, but you need to move on. Ask Jesus to heal those memories, and never let them again define who you are. You are a man or woman of God, and He loves you and NOBODY can take that away from you.

-How will God help me face my fears?
Your brain will never stop filling you with fear. Its job is to protect you, and towards that end, makes you afraid so you will confront possible danger. The Holy Spirit helps you to know when to listen to and act on your fears, and when to say "thank you very much, but I have to proceed here anyway in faith." There is an unbelievable freedom when you are able to do this. So pray constantly so that you will come to know the voice of God's Holy Spirit guiding you, or else you will be a slave of every little fear the brain fills you with.

-I was once an outgoing person, but now I am shy.
-I let people run all over me. No one takes me seriously.
-I feel like I suck at everything compared to my friends.
Will I ever do anything right?
Never let another human being determine how alive you will be.
Self-hating is a pattern of thinking, believing that you are bad, worthless, evil, unsuccessful, unlovable, or incompetent. Stop putting yourself down and comparing yourself to others. You were not born to be them. You were born to be you, and that might very well mean that you are not made to excel at the same things your friends do. Work like crazy at developing your gifts and trust the rest to God.

Where do negative beliefs about yourself come from?
The comments of others, especially our family and peers, can be very important to us, and when they are negative and rejecting, they can hurt a great deal. There is a tendency to believe what others say. It is very important to not allow your image and feelings about yourself be determined by other people. The biggest put-down artist of all ends up being ourselves, because we

have the power to repeat all those negative messages and experiences over and over again in our minds.

Some people don't need other people's torment to ruin their self-image; they make themselves feel bad by being overly perfectionistic. Strive to do and be your best; but accept the reality we are all imperfect, we all sin, and we are all loved by our Creator more than we can even imagine.

There is a freedom that comes with deciding that you will not allow your self-worth and self-image be determined by another person or your own fearful brain. Your worth is something that comes from you and your relationship with your Creator.
The past is gone. Here and now is what is real. Even though we are all growing and getting better each day, God loves us just as we are right now. God made you the way he did because he thought you might enjoy being you. So then it becomes absurd to compare ourselves to others.
-Never allow your self-image to be determined by others.
-Remember that God made you to be *you.*
-Experience yourself as constantly improving.
-Respect yourself- or no one else will respect you.
-Love your life- no one will ever be harder on you than yourself. Others will say a thing here and there. You have the power to add them all up and repeat them over and over *or* change the channel.
-Stop comparing yourself to others.
-Learn from your mistakes and then let go of the past.
-Learn to enjoy the ride.
-Each day is a new beginning & yesterday does not equal tomorrow.

In every life there is a moment when a person decides they will no longer be afraid. Let *this* be that moment. Change is possible.

With God's help you can become free of those voices in your head, and you *can* do it.

If you or someone you care about is ***constantly*** experiencing the shattering of self-esteem, get professional help.

-How can I get the strength to find out who I am? I constantly feel clueless and uncertain of myself.

Confidence comes with time and prayer. It's an internal journey. No one else knows who you really are and what you were meant to be and do; no one but you and God. Know you are beloved by God and special to Him. You are a one-of-a-kind creation, and so comparing yourself to others is a futile process. Stop doing it! Be patient with yourself, enjoy the ride- the process of self-discovery. Know that you have only one person to please in this life- your Creator.

Prison

-My cousin is in jail for beating up a gay person so bad he had to be hospitalized. I am so ashamed.
-My brother is in jail. I'm so worried for him. How can I help?
-My cousin is in jail. Is his life ruined forever?

It can be very upsetting, even horrifying to see someone you care about make such a seriously wrong decision that they end up imprisoned. You can't really change the situation, but you can be of help to them.

1- You can pray that they will be able to make the most of the situation. When surrounded by others who are also incarcerated, some people become more hardened into a criminal mentality. Others find God, and their true selves, and become motivated and prepared to make whole new lives as soon as they re-enter society. I have had young people in jail tell me that it was the best thing that ever happened to them. They say that had they not had their lives interrupted, they would have continued

down a path that would have ended with them damaged even further or maybe even dead.
2- You can write to them letting them know of your love, prayer and support. It means a great deal to them to receive these letters and cards. Corresponding gives them the chance to express themselves, and keep connected to the outside world
3- Visit them if you can

Regret
-*I never went to my grandfather's funeral.*
-*My grandpa died and I regret that I never visited. I never got to say goodbye. I wish he was still here.*
-*I wish I could have met my grandparents.*
-*I regret going too far with a boy.*
-*I'll never forgive myself for some of the things I've done. I regret so many of my decisions.*
-*My cousin died and I never told her I love her*
We cannot go back and undo the past;
 but we *can* always repent the things we regret. *And:*
-We can always ask for God's help to not repeat those things.
-We can ask His blessings on those hurt by our actions.
-Sometimes we can apologize to them,
 or even make it up to them.
Some things we cannot change.
Let God forgive you, and forgive yourself. Learn from it and move forward. Don't waste time beating yourself up.

Relationships
-*I'm in love with a guy who got his last girlfriend pregnant.*
-*What is true love?*
-*Why do guys cheat?*
-*Why can't boys control their hormones?*

-What do I do if a guys says one thing, but does another?
-How do you know if someone really loves you?
-Why do girls take relationships so seriously?
-What do you do when you love some one but they don't love you back?
-I was played, used, and I don't believe in love anymore.
-I was dumped. How do I get over my ex breaking up with me? I'm afraid I might get hurt again
-Does age really matter if you really love the person?
-I'm in a destructive, poisonous relationship and it is taking a toll on me emotionally & physically.
-I've been backstabbed so many times I don't think I can ever trust again.

Following your heart is a powerful and also at times painful experience. When we fall in love, we tend to go with our emotions, and sometimes don't listen to our better judgment. **When someone loves you, they want your happiness and well-being as much as their own.**

Girls: when it comes to guys, pay attention to what they do, more than what they say. Also, there *are* guys out there with a heart, and if you end up with one- don't play.

Guys: girls do take relationships very seriously: **never** use them or mislead them. You *can* control your hormones, and desires. Don't be a player or cheater. In the world of *real* men, you disgrace yourself.

When you recognize that a relationship is causing you more pain than joy, it's time to let it go.

Avoid Common mistakes:
1- *Don't* think that having sex will solidify the relationship and keep the person.
2- *Don't* put up with abusive behavior- don't degrade yourself.

3- *Don't* be oblivious. What they did to the ones before you, they will do to you.
4- *Don't* deny reality by denying the truth when they tell you or you see a relationship is over.
5- *Don't* overreact. Most teen dating relationship don't work out (as many as 99%).
6- *Don't* give in to the fear that you will never find happiness again in another relationship.

Running Away
-I can't deal with my family anymore. I want to run away.
     You might think that leaving your home is a good solution to whatever it is that is bothering you or hurting you with your family. It really is ***not*** a good choice. Living with friends wears out real fast for everybody. Getting a job at a young age that can pay for all your living expenses is difficult, if not impossible. Living on the streets is an ugly and dangerous life. Stealing can land you in jail. People are out there looking for you to join the pool of people they own who sell their bodies for money. You will end up being a slave to these pimps. Prostitution is a miserable life that usually leads to sickness, or even death.
Never leave home until you have a safe alternative.
So before you run away, try to find some other way to deal with your challenges. Use extended family resources or professional help.

School Challenges
-Im getting really bad grades. How do I turn this around?
Give your schoolwork everything you've got. Ask your teachers for help. Teachers appreciate it when you show an interest in doing well in their class. If you blow it on a test, ask what

you can do to make up for it or do for extra credit. it shows you care.

-I have trouble concentrating in school.

Take an honest look at your habits. Are you spending lots of nights playing video games? Cut it out. You're wasting time and destroying concentration of other things that matter far more, like your school work.

Are you getting enough sleep? It's important.

What are you eating? Are you eating a good breakfast? Do you have a healthy balanced diet? If not, make changes.

Is there somebody or something else bothering you that is keeping you from being able to focus? If so speak to a parent, friend, counselor.

-I'm really falling behind in school

Having school challenges doesn't mean you are stupid. Figure out what is going on. Is the class too advanced for you? Are you keeping up with, and doing your homework? How are your study habits? Is it something going on outside of school that is affecting you? Get help.

Sex

-What's the big deal of having sex before marriage if two people love each other?

-How do you know if your boyfriend is just using you for sex?

-Catholics are supposed to save themselves for marriage. How can I possibly do this, and not get labeled a freak? Every one my age is having sex. Why are Catholics the only people against it?

-I have sex with my boyfriend all the time. I think I'm addicted.

Catholics and Christians are *not* the only ones who say that sex outside of marriage goes against what sex is for.

Everything that God creates is for a purpose.

The purpose of sex is Life:
1- The life of a marriage - that a couple committed to each other for life can bond in love and pleasure
2- To bring new life into the world. God could have chosen to bring new life into the world any way he wanted. He chose it to happen within the complete gift of a man and woman to each other in loving commitment- body, mind, emotions and soul in the sexual act.

Temptation
-I can't stop thinking about sex.
-I masturbate too much. I am probably addicted to it.
-I think I might be addicted to porn. How can I know?
    If I am, how do I stop?

    Having sexual control is difficult, but possible. It is important to avoid sexual temptation. Don't set yourself up to be in situations, in places, or with people where it will be hard to resist. Young people today are not the first to be aroused by sexual urges, but you are the first to grow up with porn on your phone in your pocket, or with the click of a mouse on your computer. Pornography is very tempting, and very irresistible. 85% of all internet traffic is porn. That does not mean 85% of the websites are pornography. It's where 85% of people choose to go, giving you some idea of how addictive it can be. It can take hold of you, causing a need for more and more outrageousness, and it can make you unable to relate to actual human bodies who cannot compete with the airbrushed models in porn.

    If you would have been alive 100 or 200 years ago almost anywhere on earth, as puberty kicked in your parents would have made arrangements for you, and you would be married, paired up and reproducing. If you're reading this you probably live in the developed world, where preparing for a job, and making a life to support oneself and one's family requires a much longer period of specialized training; delaying the marriage, and reproducing process.

So there is an extended period where young people have all these urges, and no outlets that are acceptable in God's eyes. Does God realize this, and understand the difficulty in living up to His word in these times? Of course. Does he want to help young people maintain sexual purity? Absolutely.

There is simply no area of life that we should leave God and love out; that includes our sexuality.

-I'm being pressured to have sex. everyone in my social group is doing it.

What to do to avoid sexual temptation:

1- Pray, remember God's promise in the Bible to help you.

2- Avoid temptation- don't just wander around the internet at night, don't watch or look at porn- ever.

3- Remember- an addiction is when you can't stop, because you don't feel fully alive unless you are engaged in a behavior. If you discover you are addicted to masturbation, sex or porn, ask God's help, talk with someone you trust, get spiritual direction, speak with a counsellor who can give you coping skills, join a support group- (yes they exist).

4- Commit yourself- that you will save yourself for the person who you will spend the rest of your life with. Doing what is right for you is more important that pleasing your friends

5- Commit yourself that you will never use another human being for your quick pleasure, or to assert your manhood or womanhood. Having sex will not turn you into a man or woman. You don't have to prove anything to anyone.

6-Remember that having sex can lead to pregnancy or worse, a sexually transmitted disease, even if you just do it once. The rates of sexual disease in young people is astronomical.

7- Remember that not everyone who is claiming to be sexually active really is and having sex when you don't rally want to will feel very bad

GLBTQ issues
-I am bisexual. I am scared how people will react if they knew about the gay side of me.
-My grandmother says I'm going to hell because I am gay. Am I?
-I am always being called gay by my friends and family members.
-I am gay and everyone judges me and makes fun of me.
  Will God condemn me too?
-I'm gay. Does God hate me or not? Some say yes, some say no. It's very confusing.
-How do you deal with homophobia?
-I am so afraid to tell my father I'm gay. He might reject me forever.

No matter what your sexuality is, be and love who you are, and most of all know that God loves you for who you are, and how he made you. If anyone wants to reject you because of their homophobia, it's their problem, not yours. God not only does not hate you, He loves you the same as all His children. Anyone who He has created could not be a mistake. God simply asks that when it comes to sexual expression, gay people hold to the same rules (His Law) as everyone else; that the only people who should be having sexual relations are married couples, because they are the only ones, who fulfill what the sexual act is intended for.

Talk with someone you trust and who will understand and not judge you. That will give you the courage to tell your parents and family. Most of all no matter how many rejections you may experience, take comfort and strength in knowing that the creator of whole universe loves you.

Sexual abuse/rape

-My cousins sexually molested me, now I am anxious about everything
-How do I overcome the pain of being molested?
-I was raped for most of my life. I am suicidal and cutting and afraid nothing can change. My life is hell.
-I have been sexually abused by a family member and never told anyone about it. I don't know how to heal.
-I was abused by my father.
-I was raped when I was ten by my father's friend's son. He drugged me and I couldn't fight back. I wish I could have done something. Now I am scared to make friends and I am never happy.
-I was sexually harassed by a teacher in 8th grade.
-My school counselor was nice to me, now I find out he's a child abuser.

These experiences are among the most serious violations of a person that can happen. If you or someone you love has been sexually abused or raped:

1- You did not deserve it. Their behavior is wrong, and not related to anything you did.

2- You deserve the chance to be healed of it. Make sure a parent or guardian knows, and you get professional help.

3- If it is a parent or someone in the family who did this to you, it can be very difficult. No parent, stepparent, sibling, relative or family friend has the right to abuse you physically or sexually. You have to speak out anyway and tell a counselor or trusted person; if for no other reason, than to save someone else from having to go through what you went through. They will know what you have to do regarding the law and your family.

4- If for some reason you are not believed or supported in your family, speak with a counselor or social worker.

5- No matter what: get counseling- make sure the counselor knows specifically how to help someone who has been through what you have been through. It is very important that you deal with everything related to the abuse/rape experience. If you do not, it might poison your personality and relationships in the future.

6- call the child abuse Hotline 800-422-4453

Sibling challenges

-My sibling is always favored over me.
-My brother and I never talk. How can I strengthen our relationship, because I am afraid we will have none when we get older?
-My siblings gang up on me and don't accept me.
-I strongly disapprove of my sibling's choices.
-My sister is always mean to me & doesn't respect me for who I am.
-My sister hates me. She treats everyone better than me, who
	she treats like her worst enemy. It hurts so much.
-My brother corrupts my family.

Incidents of sibling rivalry and conflict are very common in families; but sometimes it can get out of control.

If it's a case of constant fighting or bad communication, talk with them in a calm moment. Let them know that you wish things could change, and be better. If they are making bad decisions, hurting themselves or you or the family, do the same. Talk with your parents if there is favoritism, or someone is in danger or ruining everything.

Speak with the sibling with whom there is a conflict or bad relationship. One of three things will happen:

1- They will laugh at you or ignore your request.
2- They may do better for awhile, but then go back to their old ways.
3- You might have a whole new relationship with your sibling.
It takes two people to restore and build a positive relationship, and if they do not want to, pray for them, and for you and know that you tried.

Sickness

-My dad is sick and isn't getting any better.
-My grandfather has dementia and it is affecting the whole family.
-My only living grandma is getting sick, what can I do besides pray?
-Everyone in my family is dying of cancer. I can't forget about them.
-Someone in my family had a stroke.
-My grandpa has Alzheimer's disease and doesn't even remember who I am. I miss the relationship we used to have.
-My grandpa is dying of cancer.
-My mom has breast cancer.

It is very painful to see someone you love suffer, and to feel powerless to personally heal and take away their injury or condition.

This is what you CAN do:

-Support them- visit, call, make a card. Sometimes young people avoid visiting a sick person. *"I don't want to see them like that." "I don't want to remember them that way";* and then they regret it later.
-Educate yourself and your family about the illness.
-Be brave for the patient.
-Be encouraging and let them grieve if they need to.
-Get them additional supportive help if they would like it
-Don't neglect other family members.
-Share with your church or class and think about how they can help if they ask.
-Take time for yourself away from your stress.
-Be honest with loved ones without frightening them.
-Enjoy & cherish the time you have with your loved one.
-Above all, pray for them and with them. If they don't have God in their life, it could open up a door for them.

-My father had a heart attack. After it happened he was more careful about his diet; but now he eats bad again and I am worried about losing him.
Tell him of your concerns and pray for him.

-I have asthma.

When it's you who is the one with a sickness, be it asthma, diabetes or anything else, you first accept that it is a condition you have. Don't resist or deny reality. But don't let it define you either. Seek out people your age who have dealt with your condition, and yet remain positive. Learn from them. Pray for the strength from God to face your challenge.

Smoking

-I tried to get my mother to stop smoking, and no matter how much I cry and beg- it makes no difference.
-My relative/parent is smoking and I'm afraid I'll lose them from that.
-My friend is smoking cigarettes.

It's hard to watch someone you care about doing something that you know is no good for them. You have to say something. Be prepared to possibly be ignored, or even lashed out at if it is an adult who is smoking.

Pray for them and follow these tips:
-Respect the smoker. It's their lifestyle change, and their challenge, not yours.
-Ask them if they want you to ask regularly how they're doing or not.
-Let them know they can talk with you whenever they need encouragement
-Spend time doing things with them to keep their mind off smoking
-See it from their point of view– it's hard to give up a habit
-Make your home smoke free; no one can smoke in any part of the house. Remove lighters and ash trays.
-Have faith in them. It reminds them that they *can* do it.

-Don't judge, nag, preach, tease, or scold.
-Don't take their grumpiness personally during their nicotine withdrawal (several weeks).
-Ask how you can help with the plan or program they are using.

If they slip:
-Don't assume they'll start back smoking like before. It's common.
-Remind them how long they went without a cigarette before the slip.
-Help them remember all the reasons they wanted to quit.
-Don't scold, tease, nag, blame, or make the quitter feel guilty.
-Make sure they know that you care about them whether or not they smoke.
-Remember that most people try to quit smoking several times before they succeed.
-Think of a relapse as practice. They did not fail. They are learning how to quit.
-Encourage them to try again and to learn from the attempt.

Stress/Pressure
-How do I get rid of stress of getting good grades; always having to be the best and fulfilling everyone's expectations?
-People expect so much from me and no one cares about how I feel.
-I feel so overloaded I am afraid I will explode on people.
-I get so frustrated and discouraged with school, sports and life.

Stress is part of life, so don't think you can ever get rid of it. There will always be stress in life, and some people do horrible things once obsessed with trying to remove all stress at any cost. Because it can't be eliminated, the challenge becomes dealing with the stress in your life in a healthy way.
-Face and accept reality- don't deny what's really going on
-Have an activity that gives you a physical outlet.
-Don't medicate.

-Pray the Serenity prayer. (page 12) Because stress is usually the result of frustration at not being able to change a negative situation, or accepting one that needs action, it's important to learn when you have to accept, and when you need to change something.

Stuck
-I have trouble making decisions.
-How do we change?
-How do I find what I'm looking for?
-How can I keep the motivation to achieve my dreams?
-I am afraid to share my story because they will feel bad for me and never respect me.
-When I'm upset I can't talk with anyone, because I don't want them to judge me.

It's very easy at times to get stuck; to be unable to figure out what to do next, to feel unable to get things right. If the reason you are stuck is because you are missing some crucial knowledge, then seek it out. If you are emotionally drained or stuck in a bad habit, talk with a counselor. If you are physically tired, see a doctor and look at your eating, exercise and sleeping patterns.

Look at your spiritual life: are you praying, going to church, reading the Bible, loving people? Is there something that you should be doing; a change you should make that you have been avoiding?

Being stuck is not a comfortable feeling; but it can be a good thing if, in the middle of it, you discover something new that will give your life a jumpstart.

-I go for counseling, but I don't want to talk.

If you are in a helping opportunity such as counseling, and you don't want to take advantage of it- look at why?
- is there something you're afraid to face
- have you judged that the counselor doesn't care?
- are you holding deep down beliefs that counseling is not for you?

Suicide

-I have been depressed and thinking about killing myself.
-My friend is talking about killing herself. What should I do?
-My father shot himself. I am mad at God for taking my father so soon.
-My cousin committed suicide. Is he going to hell? I feel like I am in hell, because I never saw it coming. I must have not done a good enough job of showing him how much I loved him.
-I have been hospitalized for suicidal thoughts.
-A girl in my school tried to kill herself by setting herself on fire.
-My uncle committed suicide and nothing has been good in my family since then.
-Is suicide a sin if a person was bullied really bad?

Suicide is a permanent solution to a temporary problem and it is serious. It is the second biggest killer of young people in the United States, and the police believe it is in reality number one. The person who attempts suicide, but fails, can end up crippled for life, with all of the same challenges as before. The person who commits suicide will never know the damage they caused the others who were left behind.

If you are suicidal, get help immediately. Talk with a parent about how you are feeling. If your friend is suicidal, go with them to get help. Contact a local suicide prevention hotline or center.

Since suicide is one of the worst situations you could run into, I'm including a lot of knowledge here so you are prepared:

TEEN SUICIDE

Facts:
- taking of the gift of life
- final-robs person of chance to make changes
- sharp increase among teenagers

Causes:
- bullying, peer cruelty
- breakup & instability of the family
- failure in eyes of parents
- drug & alcohol abuse
- mental disorders
- sexual abuse
- friends or family attempted or committed suicide
- glamorization of death
- recent painful life changes
- ongoing stress- parents, romantic relationships, siblings, peers
- quick fix mentality
- breakdown of values especially respect for life
- LOSS-death, pride, opportunity, special relationship

Myths & Facts:
- myth-Those who talk about it never do it.
- fact-Nearly every suicide victim attempts to communicate their pain-80% give signs
- myth-Those who commit suicide are mentally ill.
- fact-The vast majority are not. They are depressed.
- myth-Suicidal people are intent on dying.
- fact-Most are undecided and gamble on others saving them.
- myth-Once a person attempts suicide, shame and pain prevent further attempts.
- fact-4 out of 5 suicides were preceded by earlier attempts.

-myth-If a person looks happier, the danger has passed.
-fact-Most suicides occur within 3 months of improvement.
-myth-It's only a certain type of person who does it.
-fact-Suicide crosses all economic and social groups.
-myth-Once a person is suicidal, they'll always be.
-fact-Suicide is a time-limited state of mind.
-myth-suicide runs in the family. It's unpreventable.
-fact-It's individual, yet prior ones give permission.
-myth-Suicide happens with no warning.
-fact-Many clues are usually given.

Warning signs:
-suicide note
-depression and a deep sense of hopelessness
-running away from home
-persistent boredom, passive apathetic behavior
-complaint about physical symptoms emotionally related- headaches, stomachaches, fatigue
-decline in school performance
-preoccupation with death themes
-radical personality & mood changes
-verbal expression of own death
-increased drug & alcohol abuse
-history of physical, emotional, mental or sexual abuse
-verbal clues and revealing statements- "I won't be a problem for you much longer". "it's no use", "Nothing matters anymore"
-sudden interest in risk-taking and dangerous activity, reckless driving, owning/using weapons
-self mutilation
-anniversaries of traumatic events
-giving away or throwing out valued possessions
-making out a will
-increased irritability and behavior problems

-depression resulting from loss of important person or thing
-history of previous suicide attempts
-inattention to physical hygiene
-frequent sleeping disorders or complaints
-recent withdrawal from therapeutic treatment
-sudden lifting of severe depression
-rebelliousness, belligerence, violent aggressive activity
-excessive guilt
-loss of pleasure in life
-excessive fantasy life
-compulsive behaviors
-loss of interest in previously enjoyed activities
-noticeable changes in sleep and appetite patterns
-increased social withdrawal
-less interest in, loss of, or lack of friends
-history of disabilities and failure
-fear of separation
-inability to concentrate

How to help:
-Don't act as though it isn't serious.
-Don't promise to not tell anybody. Confidentiality is sacred, except for when someone's life is in danger. They do not have the right to ask you to promise not to reveal their suicide plan.
-Active Listen-show you care and are concerned.
-Emphasize temporary nature of most situations; suicide is a permanent solution to a temporary challenge.
-To determine degree of risk ask direct questions:
"Have you ever attempted taking your life?"
If they have they, they could easily do so again.
"Have you thought about how you would do it?"
If they have a plan, they are close to doing it.

- Do not leave them without a promise that they will not take their life before speaking with you or someone else. If they will not promise, do not let them out of your sight and get help immediately.
- If you feel their life is at stake, don't promise to keep the conversation a secret.
- Reassure them that suicidal thoughts are not abnormal, merely unhelpful- many teens think about it.
- Define and clarify the situation and possible non-life-threatening solutions.
- Remember you don't have to have all the answers. Seek out someone who knows more than you or your family and friends.
- Avoid provoking further guilt.
- Contact police, professional assistance or responsible adult if in immediate danger, and remove all lethal objects.
- Help them arrive at a plan of action to deal with their situation.
- Stay calm and avoid minimizing their suicidal thoughts or plans.
- Encourage the sharing of feelings.
- Emphasize better alternatives to suicide.
- Set up a future meeting to evaluate progress.
- Call teen suicide hot line 800-621-4000 or a local support person.
- Pray for, and with, your friend.

If someone in your family has committed suicide, it can devastate those left behind. It usually becomes crucial for such a family to receive professional help toward their healing.

The Church no longer teaches that people who commit suicide go to hell; which is not to say that it *isn't* seriously wrong.

Violence

-Why is it that people are violent?
-Why are there bad people in the world?
-I play violent video games a lot. Is there anything wrong with that?
-My little brother is suffering. He's always getting hurt by my dad.
-Is it wrong to wish evil on someone who has done wrong to you multiple times and refuses to change?
-I fantasize about killing my father who makes everyone's life miserable.
-My brother is physically violent.
-Two of my closest friends have died in violent and freaky ways. I have begun to look at the world as a dangerous place.

1- God gives us freedom to commit love or to commit violence. The capacity for violence is hard-wired into humans; it's part of our animal survival instincts. Jesus gives us for all time the example of radically responding to violence by refusing to hurt back. Jesus shows us that He, and those who follow Him, break the chain of violence by refusing to return it. *"The cycle stops with me."*

There is also the Christian belief that we have a right to defend ourselves, and those we love with force if necessary. Clearly violence is the least acceptable solution. It has been said "violence is the last refuge of the unimaginative." Only those who cannot come up with a more creative solution will resort to violence.

2- There is no place where violence can't occur. Still, be smart. Don't set yourself up to be in dangerous, violent situations. In New York City there was recently several different incidents of tragic rape/murders of young women in their twenties. They certainly did not deserve what happened to them. Nonetheless in each case they had been drinking heavily in bars all night. They were walking down dark side streets between 3 and 5 in the morning, and were severely drunk.

3- Violence in your home is not to be tolerated. If you are getting nowhere with trying to put an end to the suffering of violence in your home; make sure you talk with a counselor or social worker.

4- If you return violence with violence, and this includes cursing them, and wishing evil on them, then you have let your enemy drag you down to their level. It is completely natural to be angry at someone who is treating you or someone you love with violence. If you are feeling the desire to strike back, don't react. Take time to sort out your options, and who you can speak with about your situation.

-There are violent kids in my school. One has the locker next to mine and I feel threatened. What should I do?

Let an adult know you feel endangered.

Get your locker moved.

Defend yourself if necessary.

If transferring to a less violent school is an option, you and your parents should consider it.

Faith Questions & Situations

Afterlife

What is hell like?

Hell is separation from God and love, in this life and in the next. At the moment of death, we are with God, and there is a review or judgment of your life. Certainly hell would be realizing that you had this glorious opportunity of an earthly life, to participate in the privilege of miraculous giving and receiving of love, and blew it by only worrying about yourself. We don't know for sure if at the moment of death, upon encountering the infinite love and mercy of God, anyone chooses to persist in their rejection of Him, and of love. We know that there were spiritual beings, who were in God's immediate presence, who chose to reject Him. This means that even being with God in all His power and glory, the choice to reject it exists. Still, we do not judge with certainty if anyone besides those fallen angels is definitely in Hell.

-I'm afraid I'll never be good enough for heaven.
-What do I have to do to go to heaven?

You can stop worrying. You'll NEVER be good enough for heaven. Heaven is being with the Creator of the universe, who is perfect. You know that you are not. None of us are. At your moment of death, you will never be able to demand that heaven be given to you, because of your worth or accomplishment. Heaven is a gift. It cannot be deserved, earned, or bought. It is a gift made possible by Jesus' act of self-sacrificing love on the cross. Sacrificial love is the only hope humanity ever has.

-Is there any hope for an atheist to make it to heaven?

People who never came to God in this life for whatever reason, or of no fault of their own, but who lived lives beyond the scope of their self-concern, and full of loving are lifted up by Jesus to the Creator in heaven.

-My grandmother always says "offer it up for the souls in purgatory" What the heck is she talking about? What do people do i n purgatory? Is it true that prayers help you go to heaven? And if God is so merciful, why doesn't He just let everyone into heaven?

Purgatory is a real place and state where souls that are not ready for heaven go. It is for people who did not reject God, but whose lives fell seriously short. Think of it as summer school. You know you're moving on to the next grade, but there are some things you have to learn, and take care of first.

Because all of reality is connected, the prayers of the living, and those in heaven do affect those who are in purgatory. They are not earning their right to go to heaven. We can never be good enough to deserve it. It's in Jesus that we are saved. They just need to work some things out so they can better receive the gift that heaven is.

As for God just letting everyone into heaven, he is merciful, but also just, and what would the value of heaven be if our earthly life didn't matter?

-Isn't bringing flowers to a grave ridiculous since they are not really there?

The person who has passed away, and is now in the afterlife is not hanging around under or near their grave; but in their spiritual state, they do know of our feelings, and our actions, so they really are touched by this tradition of honoring.

Of course this beautiful and loving gesture of giving flowers is best done while people are still living in their bodies.

-What will heaven be like? Sitting on clouds playing harps doesn't sound like much fun.

No it certainly doesn't! Those images of peace and phrases like "eternal rest" came in times when people struggled through physically harsh and tiring lives. Heaven for them was seen as finally getting a break from so much hard work and constant struggle. Heaven is being completely one with the Creator, who is infinitely, lovingly creating, and would be eternal happiness.

Changing the world

-The world is so screwed up, how am I supposed to help people?
-How can a person who is young make a difference in this world?
-How can the world change for the better?

How? Through prayer and love united in faith in Jesus. Prayer is important because in prayer your thoughts are connected to God's thoughts. Love is important because in love your actions are connected to God's actions. Faith in Jesus is important because human effort alone is not enough to shift things; it must happen on the spiritual level.

There is no such thing as an insignificant act of love.

No prayer is wasted. All loving, prayerful, sacrificial acts affect the entire physical and spiritual reality.

Church concerns

-I understand lots of children and teens were molested by Catholic priests, and nothing was done. How can you expect me to take a religion that would allow that to happen seriously?

It was a horrific tragedy, and you have every right to be disgusted and outraged. The children should have been protected in the first place, and more people in powerful positions should have been held accountable. It was illegal, and morally wrong, and will always be inexcusable. Sexual abuse has occurred in almost every institution where adults were working with children; churches, schools, scouting organizations, and most of all, families. It is always wrong.

Ever since this scandal broke, the Catholic Church has been doing all it can to protect young people. There are new rules and procedures in place that mean that many more people are aware of danger signs, now making it much more likely this tragedy should never happen again.

-Why doesn't the church accept everyone when God does?

Yes, when the church only focuses on the rules, and not loving people they come across as judgmental and non-accepting and that hurts a lot of people. No one should feel they are unloved and not accepted by God because of the Church. God loves and accepts everyone He creates, while not approving of everything they do. Humans are free to choose to follow God's law or reject it. The Church's job is to make sure people know what God's law is. They sometimes fail to remember that we are all sinners, and forget to embrace people, be their friend, and support them as they try to live a good life; which can be more difficult for some than others.

-The only thing the Catholic Church cares about is gay marriage-. Why?
It certainly has seemed that way for too long. The church is upholding it's consistent teaching that the sexual act is to be for a man and a woman. I agree that there are so many more important things that the church should be speaking about, and as of the second edition of this book, Pope Francis has been moving to correct this.

-How come the church has all it's riches when people are starving. It's hypocritical and wrong.
Not nearly enough is done to alleviate human suffering. It can be very frustrating to see churches in the US redecorating,

while other churches are worshipping in straw huts; and worse than that, all over the world, even in wealthy countries, there are people who are sick and starving.

Remember that no institution has done, or does more to help people who suffer than the Catholic Church. Catholic and Christian groups are operating at the grassroots level all over the world to help people who are struggling and suffering. I have seen it with my own eyes.

The wealth that the Vatican holds is in real estate and artistic treasures that they store for, and share with, all the world. Also know that the average Catholic parish is usually scraping pennies together to keep Jesus' message and work going at the local level.

Pope Francis is someone who would agree with you. He picked his name to honor St. Francis of Assisi, who is known as the saint of the poor. Pope Francis refuses to sit on thrones, wear expensive clothing, or even live in the Pope's palace. He is constantly reaching out to, and speaking on behalf of, the poor. I pray that his example will spread out throughout the church and the whole world.

Doubt

-If there really is a creator, don't you think he'd be really disgusted with what we've done to his creation?

God is constantly creating, and offers us the chance to be part of it by being co-creators. Imagine giving and giving so much to somebody and all they ever do is trash it, or use it for their own advantage.

God hasn't given up on us. He continually sends new life into the world, and that includes you; and each individual and generation have a choice to make: "culture of death" or "civilization of love"?

-What if I don't really think God is real? When will I feel Him?
-I keep hearing that religion is just a manmade way of trying to control people. Tell me why I shouldn't believe that it's true.

All religions are human beings' way of expressing their connection to something bigger than themselves. Certainly throughout human history individuals and groups of people have used religion as a means to control others. It is also true that some people prefer to be led like sheep, and fall right into those manipulative kinds of people's plans.

This does not mean that religion exists only for this purpose. Countless people have found in their religion the inspiration and spiritual strength to live noble lives, and create tremendous goodness and beauty in this world, and none of this is negated by some people's abuses.

How close you are to God and How real he is has nothing to do with our feelings at any time. He is closer to us than we are to ourselves

-How can I follow a religion that is represented by a book that could possibly have been made up?

The Catholic/Christian faith is not about a book; its foundation is a relationship, a relationship with the Savior of the world. Jesus Christ really can be known, and experienced. The Bible is our Holy Book, and God can be known through it; but He is also in the sacraments, especially in the Eucharist, the Church, our hearts, our lives, and our world.

-I want to believe, but my head says go with science.

Your brain is always going to go with science. The brain functions as a computer, and its job is to protect you from any perceived danger. So it is oriented towards what your senses perceive; looking for signals that something or someone may be of danger to you. While the effects of the spiritual world are visible, it itself is not; and so your brain will ignore it or treat it as a dream. What's important to do is remember that you are not your brain. You are the one who operates it, just as you are the one who operates the computer. Prayer is the way you tap into the spiritual world. If you never make time for prayer and silent reflection in your life, you will become addicted to your senses, and limited to the world they perceive.

I have seen some youtube videos exposing Christianity, and especially the Catholic religion, as a fraud.

Yes, there are a lot of videos. Most of them have a little bit of truth in them; and a lot of other half-truths or even lies. I don't want to take the time to dispute individual ones here, but I encourage you to also watch the youtube videos or read books, which specifically answer charges made in atheist books and videos.

I wish I could believe in God, but I can't understand why He allows so much pain. Doesn't He care?

He cares very much; His Sacred Heart constantly breaks. God values freedom. He will not interfere in human choices, or with the physical level breaking down. The cycle of birth, death and new life are consistent throughout His creation, and so with human life as well.

Humans rebelled against God, and that opens the door for sin to build on itself over generations into a systemic evil. There are also spiritual beings in our reality who also do not serve the creator and they are also in the mix.

God does care deeply; and so in the midst of all this he sends His Son into the world to free us from these sins and offering us eternal life with Him. This life with God in heaven is free from the suffering that everyone, including Jesus, experienced in human life.

My grandma was a very religious person, but when she got cancer she thought God had abandoned her. She blamed God and lost faith and won't talk with or see anyone now.

It's very sad that someone had faith all her life, and then when she needed it most, lost it. She may have thought that being religious would save her from the really bad things that can happen in life, and now she is angry and feeling betrayed. It doesn't work that way. Some of the most faithful followers of God suffer the most. Pray for your grandmother. Reach out to her, and let her know that God has not abandoned her. Everyone suffers in this life, even Jesus did, and He knows what she feels and is going through it with her.

Faith
What is the most important thing we have to do regarding our faith?

Jesus told us: Love God, and love our neighbor as ourself.

Is so much going wrong in the world happening because fewer people believe in God?

Yes. We simply do not live the way God intended us to. There is also great evil and tremendous apathy at work.

-Defending my faith is really hard in school. Teachers and friends are always attacking the Church and the Christian faith. It's overwhelming and sometimes I just feel helpless. Should we be God-freaks at our young age?
-Most religious people I know are either dull, or judgmental or annoying. If I follow God will that happen to me? If so, I'm out. I don't want to be like that.

I don't blame you.
People are attracted to religion for different reasons:

-If it's because religion gives them order in the midst of chaos, they will express it in a regimented way.
-If their view of the world is negative, they may express their faith with a judgmental focus.
-If they are simply getting older, slowing down, and no longer living life in an adventurous way, they might appear boring.
-If they were once lost and now found, they may want everyone to find what they now have, and go about expressing their faith in an annoying, pushy style.

None of these approaches have to be you. A fully alive, joyful, passionate life with God is not only possible, it is what God wants for you. Never let human weakness drive you from God. Don't ever let joyless or unbelieving people keep you from wanting and living the most beautiful thing a person can have: a personal relationship with the Creator and Redeemer of the world.

-What happens to people who don't believe in God?
-Can you get to heaven without being Catholic or belonging to a church?
-God is not in my family. My mother is an atheist, and is miserable. I feel bad for her, but I don't want to be like her.
I'm worrying those I love will fall into sin, darkness and death.

God reads the heart and soul of every person, and that determines what happens after their death. As for while they are still alive, you can make a difference by modeling for them the joy and strength that come from a life in the Holy Spirit. Let them see in you what knowing and serving the love of God looks like.

Pray for them; for an awakening of a hunger for God in their lives. Pray that someone will come into their life, if not you, then someone else, who, when the right moment comes, will guide and support them to make a change.

Following God
-How can I open up more and express myself to God & others?
-How do I stay on track with God?

Ask Jesus to heal and open up your heart. Do something everyday to strengthen your friendship with Jesus:
-pray
-read the Bible
-read other spiritual books
-love people
-forgive
-be grateful
-Eucharist
-Reconciliation

> *He who gains His life will lose it. He who gives His life for me will find it.*
> *Jesus*

"Live, Love, Laugh."

How do I get my friend back on the path of God?
St Francis said "preach the Good News at all times. Use words if necessary."

1- Witness to them the strength and joy that knowing and loving and serving God gives you.

2- Be ready for when a God- moment pops up where you may have the chance to share your faith verbally with them. Speak with strength, love, and respect. Ask for and trust in Jesus to give you the words and show you the moments. Never argue. No one ever came to God because they lost an argument.

3- Pray for them. This way you are part of their coming to God, even if you are not the immediate instrument.

Forgiveness

-I have been hurt and disrespected; but I have also hurt and disrespected a lot of other people. Will God forgive me for the hurt I have caused?
-I'm conceited and selfish- I'm the worst. Is there no hope for me?

Anything you are sorry for is forgiven. God does not live in the past, or hold grudges. These are human actions. Sometimes the hardest person to forgive is yourself. Repent, and then let it go; knowing that God understands, and has already forgotten it and forgiven you. Ask His help to strengthen you to never make that decision again to harm another; no matter how badly you have been hurt.

-Is it wrong to wish evil on someone who has done wrong to you many times and refuses to change?

Yes, it is always wrong to wish evil. It *is* OK to forgive them, and also decide that you are not going to allow them to hurt you over and over, and with no remorse. Doing that does not honor yourself or them. Pray about what to do. We are supposed to forgive, but there comes a time when it is no longer healthy to allow the abuse to continue.

-How do I forgive someone and get rid of the pain I feel they caused me? I am so bad at letting go of grudges and I am watching myself become a bitter person.
-I'll never forget or forgive what they did to me

Forgive, let it go. So much mental and physical illness results from the refusal to forgive, and let go of life's hurts. Remember that forgiveness is in no way saying that what they did to us was Ok. It WASN'T. It is NOT saying it *didn't* matter- IT DID. What you are doing in forgiving is letting go of that person and what they did to you; allowing God to take care of it, while freeing yourself of the effects of bitterness and resentment. It is a great gift you give yourself. If you don't let go, it will cause you infinite more suffering than the person who hurt you.

-My grandpa died because of a doctor's mistake. How do I get past wanting to kill him for what he did to my grandpa?
One of my best friends died from a heart surgeon's mistake, so I know something of what you feel. The anger is natural to feel, but obviously you should not act on it. Bring the hurt and anger to God, and yes, forgive that doctor. Holding on to hate will not hurt him, it can only hurt you, by poisoning your heart. This is not saying what that doctor did was OK. If you look at it that way, you will never be able to let it go, because you will be believing that you are betraying your grandpa. Your grandpa would never want you to be filled with hate. Hopefully he is with God now. Ask him to pray for you to be able to let it go.
(That young doctor went on to become a world-class heart surgeon, and ironically, many years later saved my father's life!)

-What mistakes are unforgivable?
None. There is nothing you have ever done or will ever do that will cause God to withhold his love and mercy

-How do I forgive myself?
By remembering that God has forgiven you, it is pointless and ridiculous to hold onto your sins and mistakes. Let it go.

-I hurt my friend and they will not forgive me. What do I do?
If you have asked for forgiveness, and a chance to regain their trust, and they refuse, all you can do is pray for them.

Life

-I am a child born of in-vitro fertilization, and I know the church doesn't approve of this. What am I supposed to do with this? I feel like I shouldn't exist or that I am loved less by God.
You are not loved by God any less than anyone else. God desires you to be here and to be who you are. You are not a freak, and not a mistake. Love your life.

-Does what we do on this earth matter?
Absolutely! What we do on this earth matters very much. Our actions here affect our state in the afterlife.

-I once heard a priest say that we're not supposed to care about this world; it's the next life that matters. Do you agree?
I think he was probably trying to convey that we are not supposed to live as if this world is all there is. We are supposed to remember that we were made not for this world, but for heaven. This life is a small, but important, chapter in the journey of our souls.

At the same time; earth is a beautiful gift. Life here is an amazing, one of a kind creation of God, where he can bring new souls to grow and develop during human lifetimes. We have a responsibility to protect and preserve that gift.

-Are we intentionally created or randomly occurring?
If the universe and life itself are chaotic, accidental occurrences, then no. If the universe is the product and design of an intelligent creator (and increasingly scientists in every field are coming to this conclusion) then yes. Life reveals that everything created exists for a purpose. Therefore, human life and specifically your own personal life, and our collective life have a purpose. The purpose of human life is the giving and receiving of love.

-Did human beings come to earth together?
-Are we all connected or not?

These are the kinds of questions that I wish I would get asked more frequently on my retreats, because I know that if you dare to ask them and seek the answers to them, it can change your life.

While appearing separate and living separate existences, on the spiritual level, we are all connected. Science has also proven that on the most basic level, we and all of life are all one.

-I am scared about this world and the future.

Yes, I understand; it *is* very crazy out there. Things seem to be getting worse; not better. So much so, that if you don't anchor yourself in God, you could lose it.

There is a saying "trust the future to God- He is already there." Because God exists outside of time and space, He knows how this all turns out, and no matter what, He prepares a place with Him in heaven for those who are faithful to love.

We are conceived by God in love, carried by His love throughout our earthly life, and enter the afterlife across a bridge of divine love.

The world is in God's hands; not yours. Live and love in the present moment- it is all that is real, and all that matters. The past is gone, and the future is not reality yet. Pray to discover what is the unique way is which God wants to co-create love through and with you in this earthly life; and entrust the rest to Him.

Life Mission

-I feel like God might be calling me to follow him all the way,
  but I'm afraid to answer the call.

Yes, that would be unsettling. There is really only one prayer worth offering "Lord, may your will be done in my life and in this world." Be willing to say to Jesus that you will not deny Him anything; and you will live the most rewarding life you can imagine. We are all called to follow Him all the way. If all the way for you means to be a priest, deacon or sister or another form of a lifetime of ministry to others, know that He will give you the strength to be true to that calling; and that His love will be enough to sustain you. It is possible of course to follow Him all the way in other ways- Pray to find yours. Every day discover your gifts and explore what is your unique mission; **and never doubt that you have one.**

Prayer of St Ignatius
Lord Jesus Christ, take all my freedom, my memory, my understanding, my entire will. All that I have and cherish, you have given me. I surrender it all to be guided by your will. Your grace and your love are enough for me. Give me these, Lord Jesus, and I ask for nothing more.

-How and when do you find out what you are supposed to do with your life?
-I have no idea what God's plan is for me. Does he even have one?
-I want to make a difference in the world, but I feel so useless

These are most likely teenagers who wrote these; and it would be OK to not fully know the answers to these questions. I would say that the way to proceed is to pray constantly. Each day wake up, and ask God to show you during the day what you should be learning and doing. Some people get a very clear sense of exactly what they are supposed to do with their life when they're young. Some people have a general sense, and take it gradually through their high school and college/ young adult years. Others have no clue until even later. Still others have several different missions for different times in their lives.

Definitely in your high school/teen years your main job is to discover what God made you good at and exploring what he might have made you for.

Love
-No matter how much I do for others- they never do anything for me.

It hurts a lot to be used. If you are feeling this way because you believe your love should be returned, you don't have to go there. You can choose to focus on the pure joy of giving to others; the pure exhilaration of giving without concern for what is being returned.

At the same time, it's not healthy for anyone in a relationship when the giving is all one-sided. Pray about what to do: continue to give, or lovingly leave behind people who really don't care about you. Make sure you don't hold on to any hatred or resentment.

Mary
-I heard that Mary, Jesus' Mother has been appearing around the world. Isn't this just wishful thinking, or mass hallucinating by a bunch of overly religious people?

It turns out that she really has. The occurrences are too many to mention here or to ignore. I have done enough research on this subject to know that the ones that are proclaimed by the Church to be authentic are investigated thoroughly. Of course, Catholics are not required to believe in them; but the Apparitions of Mary are a great example of God's love for us. I have written a book about the apparitions called "Full of Grace- the second greatest story (n)ever told- an exploration of the Apparitions of the Virgin Mary" It is available at Amazon or you can get one from "Hope for the Children Foundation".

Morality
-How can I know right from wrong?
God both made us with he ability to know right from wrong (our reason and conscience), and He also has given us guidance. the 10 commandments are a code of the minimal that human beings must do to live a decent life. Jesus later clarified and simplified the code with one word: love. We are to love God and our neighbor as ourselves. Jesus also gave us the beatitudes, which describe a life lived in the spirit of God.

Occult
Why is our religion against witchcraft?
The Catholic faith is against anything that involves relying on another power or rituals to obtain power instead of placing our trust in God directly. Occult rituals, and even something that might seem as harmless as a Ouija board, can open the door to evil; because whenever someone seeks power that is not theirs to have, you open up a portal where evil rushes in.

Other Religions
-My aunt says "don't you dare marry a non-Christian; you'll never be happy." I think she's a little fanatic.
Knowing that every couple has to decide in which religion they will raise their children, maybe she is trying to save you that conflict. The most important thing that makes a good marriage, and a good, strong, and happy family, is when the husband and wife know how to love.

This is not being "in love." Love is working for the good of another person as much as you work for your own good. Some other religions don't emphasize this; and no matter what religion a person was raised in or follows, you will never be happy with a person who does not know how to give. Many people today, even in Catholic families, do not think about giving to others, or to put another person ahead of themselves and their own comfort or convenience. This is far more important than the religion they follow. It is also what God cares about the most: love above everything.

-If God meant for everyone to follow Jesus, why did he allow so many other religions to spring up all over the world and become so strong?

Good question. It certainly would have been easier for the world to come together through and in Christ if so many different paths had not evolved over the years. Each culture across the earth has grown in its own way. The Creator is expressing Himself uniquely, in the ways races and cultures and societies have evolved. Each has their own unique beauty, and their ugliness. All true religions and philosophies reveal something of the eternal God; but no religion ever had a founder or central figure who claimed to be the Chosen One, who would reveal the Creator. No other historical figure ever claimed to bring God to man; and heaven to earth. Only Jesus.

Humans are connected as one body; one social organism. Life shows us that every social organism: including family, team, church, school, business needs a leader to function properly. Humanity as a whole needs a leader as well. Only one person that ever lived on this earth claimed to be that leader, and that is Jesus. So no matter what religious customs and beliefs have sprung up across the world, each culture was meant to find its fulfillment in Jesus.

There are so many Christian groups and churches; how can I possibly know which one is the right one?

The division among the Christian churches is the most scandalous thing on the earth. That the Church, the friends, followers and family of Jesus, who came to bring the whole world together to the Creator, should be so divided, and often even intolerant of each other is an abomination. Jesus wants all His followers to be one body, His body; a united witness of His love to the world.

There is only one Christian Church that can trace it's roots all the way back to Jesus himself, and the apostles Jesus prepared and commissioned to continue His mission after he would leave: the Catholic Church.

Have there been serious mistakes that people in the Catholic Church have made over the years? Absolutely. The Church is made of people, who can do hideous things at times. But it's time to come back together, and the common ground will be, "They'll know we are Christians by our love."

-My Christian friends make fun of me. They say that as a Catholic I worship statues and pictures.

Catholics do NOT worship statues, photos or any other artifacts. These objects help us to focus on the spiritual; in the same way that looking at a photograph of a loved one helps us more clearly to focus on the person the photograph calls to mind.

Prayer
-I prayed for someone to not die, but they did. Why?
-I prayed; my uncle didn't get better.

Pray for one thing: for God's will to be done. Simply, a fact of life, a harsh reality is that everyone you will ever love will die, and sickness comes into almost every life.

-Why is it that when I pray nothing changes?
-When you pray and ask for a sign; how do you know you got it?
I never know for sure.
Be patient. Ask God for a sign, if it be His will; but above all, be willing to trust. God knows what we need, more than we do, and answers every prayer in one of three ways

    1- "you got it"
    2- "not now"
    3- (feels like a no)- "I've got something better in mind"

-When you are praying, how do you know it's God's voice and not just you making something up in your head?
    The more you pray, the more you become familiar with the unique way that God speaks to you. Make more time for prayer, and you will learn how to discern His voice from your own, and the many other voices that run through your head and all around you.

I pray for everyone, but not myself. Is it selfish to pray for yourself?
    Only if your needs are all you ever pray for. While prayer is not a shopping list we give to God, it's *important* to know that He wants to bless and help you with what you are going through. Bring him your needs, trusting in his will, to be done in your life.

Priorities
-How can I be close to God, but still do what I want to do?
-How can I make time for God when I am so busy?
-I have three separate lives: I am a good, well-behaved student, I am bisexual, and I get high. I seem to be able to juggle all three, but I'm worried it might hurt my life with God someday.

It can seem very exciting to be living a life where you do whatever you want; but living a divided life WILL eventually catch up with you. While it is true that you *can* do many things; **the important question** is: "what is the *right thing* to do?" What feels good, is not always the right thing. Being sexual active, smoking weed, and drinking can certainly FEEL good at the time, and even seem very natural, or not that important.

Ultimately you will have to decide who you belong to, and who you will serve. Integrity is key and as long as you play in three worlds, you have none.

Truth is more important than how you feel.

Human beings have a strong desire for the altered states that sex, drugs and alcohol provide. They have nothing to offer that is greater that all the gifts that come from having God at the center of your life. Nothing should be more important for us than God, and the condition of our soul and our readiness to meet Him at the moment of death.

-I like getting high. Is this going to hurt my life with God?
If so, why didn't Jesus say anything about it?

Everyone has to decide who, and what they will serve. The fact that you are questioning that getting high might hurt your relationship with God means that you care about it, and are afraid doing drugs might hurt it. Yes it will. Getting high gives the illusion of well-being. When you and God are flowing together- that's the real thing. Getting high on a regular basis ***will*** interfere with you being able to get there naturally. Using drugs and alcohol directly alter our perception of reality; how we see the world. Unless used for medical reasons, when we consume drugs we are essentially telling God is that the reality He has made is not good enough for us; and that we are going to take control in order to feel pleasure.

As far as *why Jesus didn't say anything about it:* there are a lot of things that Jesus did not address directly (sex is another one). What believers do, is take the Gospel values He was clear about, and apply them to life as it evolves over history. What Jesus IS very clear about is that we should allow nothing to come between us, and doing God's will in this world.

-Is it bad to love sports more than anything else?
It's a good thing to be passionate about something and give your whole self to doing it as well as you can. Sports can provide an arena for you to do that; but nothing should ever come before loving God and others. There are athletes who are able to combine all three: passionate, excellent play, love for God, and love for their teammates. (Tim Tebow, Jeremy Lin, Seattle Seahawks, and many others.)

-I have a great life. I'm really selfish and I can't let God in.
The way your life is going can only lead to one thing: a moment when you will regret living this way. Why is it that you can't (won't) let God in? You mention your selfishness, and that makes sense. Let it go now before you hurt yourself or worse someone you care about, because of it. Know that Jesus is knocking at the door of your heart; and just because you have not let Him in before does not mean that He will now hold it against you.

Sacraments
-My priest says that communion really is the actual body and blood of Jesus. Does he really expect me to believe that?
Yes, this is a tough one, but it is our faith because it comes from Jesus Himself. When He said it, many people stopped following Him, saying it was too hard to believe *(and that was Jesus saying it!).* We believe the Eucharist really is Je-

sus present in His body, blood, soul and divinity because He Himself revealed it. Knowing that many have trouble with believing, Jesus has blessed us with over 100 miracles where He reveals His power and presence. I have written a book called *"Living Bread"* covering all of those miracles, and other miraculous phenomena related to the Eucharist if you're interested.

-God forgives me. Isn't that enough? Why go to Confession?

God does forgive every sin. When we sin, it is not just between us and God; we also hurt other people. Jesus knew that as humans we need a human touch. In the sacrament of Reconciliation (Confession) the priest represents God and the community we have hurt; and so you experience the forgiveness of God and the community.

A daily review at the end of your day, is a helpful habit to get into. No doubt it will reveal both your loving actions, as well as all the things you can bring to God for forgiveness.

Participating in the sacrament of Reconciliation when you've committed chronic or serious sin is important. Since getting yourself to this sacrament can be challenging, God rewards it with extra graces to help you sin less.

Suffering

-I doubt God's existence because of all the terrible things that have happened.
-How does God let horrible things happen if He is all powerful and almighty?
-How can God expect you to believe in him when your whole life is a disappointment?
-I prayed, my uncle didn't get better. Later for God.
-Is it OK to question God after something bad happens?
-Why does God allow diseases to exist in the world?

*-What kind of God lets wars, genocides and natural disasters happen? Not a God **I** feel like worshipping and following!*

You would have to be oblivious *not* to ask these questions. The world today is the result of what human beings have done with the way God has set things up. We are made by a loving Creator, who values freedom and love. He will not restrict our freedom, and He will not force us to love. The world is a gift given to us from God to create with Him an expression of the heaven we are going home to; or not.

We humans have animal instincts that we can channel and control, or indulge. We have souls, which can allow to overflow into life, or can shut down and die. Suffering is always the result when we choose to follow our animal instincts without letting them be guided by God.

The bottom line is that humans rejected God, and since then have set two things in motion:

1- a rejection of God ingrained in human society; where one sin builds on the next, and becomes entangled and ingrained, and grows like cancer.

2- the physical reality is constantly breaking down. Human bodies break down and eventually die. The physical world is in upheaval connected to the deterioration of human life. The two are connected.

In the midst of this, God brings His Son into the world, and by His sacrifice we are saved from everlasting effects of this deterioration.

The evils that you object to are not the end of the story.

There is a victory over sin and death and suffering.

We inhabit a redeemed, but unfinished, world.

The God you question is waiting at the door of your heart inviting you to join in with Him in the adventure of loving.

Pain is not the only way to God, but it is the most definite, because in one form or another, it comes into every human life. Because human beings can be so full of themselves and believing they do not need God, it is the suffering in life that knocks us down from our own pedestals.

Because of sin (man's choices to reject God and His law of love), and the breaking down of the physical world, suffering is inevitable in this life.

Of course it is OK to let our anger, hurt and frustration when you, your loved one, or anyone, suffers. But it is important not to get stuck there.

-Why does God let bad things happen to good people?
-Why does God do bad things to good people?

God **allows** suffering to happen to good people; He does not **do** bad things to people. They are two different things. Being a good person does not protect you from suffering. Remember Jesus is God's Son, the best person who ever lived. Yet, He endured the most vicious torture, and painful way of killing, that humans have ever devised. He was teaching us that suffering comes into every life; it's what we do with it that matters. Jesus showed us what to do with suffering: go through it, because a resurrection is waiting.

God gets no joy from watching anyone suffer. He chooses to go through our human suffering with us, and in the midst, work though loving and courageous people to heal the wounds.

You meet a lot of kids our age. What do you think it is that our age group needs most?

God. In this respect your generation is no different than any other. All human beings have been created in such a way that we are not complete, not really our true selves, unless we are connected to and immersed in our Creator.

Regarding the times you are living in, this is a time of intense systematic enslavement of many by a few. Young people are getting caught up in it, not questioning and not aware of the bigger picture of the gradual erosion of our humanity. Young people also pay the greatest price of the sickness of a loss of love and respect for life. There is a killing off of the human spirit and I see it manifesting in:
-addiction to technology
-medication of the masses
-overstimulation through media and pornography
-economic injustice and imbalance
-the destruction of the environment
-the slaughter of the young
-the many forms of slavery that still exist
-loss of contact with nature
-isolation in families and within society
-profound loneliness and social withdrawal
-not caring about the future, fear of failure to change
-lack of passion, intimacy and effort
-sense of entitlement and lack of gratitude
-lack of silence and ability to pray or even desire to pray
-a loss of civility, respect and empathy
-increased passivity and victim mentality
-lack of appreciation of and wasting of food and resources
-wasting time, mindless distractions and inability to focus
-preoccupation with triviality and celebrity
-focus on conformity rather than creativity
-addiction to pleasure and convenience
-loss of willingness and ability to work hard
-imprisonment of masses, loss of privacy, massive surveillance
-systematic enslavement of humanity and erosion of freedoms
-loss of community and belonging

Conclusion

Egg, carrot, & coffee beans
Place an egg, a carrot, and some coffee beans into three separate pots of boiling water. After boiling them a while, notice what has happened.

The carrot started out hard; but the heat makes it soft causing it to wilt, lose strength.

The egg started out soft, and malleable inside; but it turns out hard and stiff on the inside.

The coffee beans change the hot water into coffee. When heated, they release their fragrance and flavor.

Which are you when challenges arise, when adversity occurs, when the heat is on? The egg, carrot or coffee?
Do you get weak like the carrot?
Do you become hardened like the egg?
Or are you like the coffee bean; when things are at their worst, the hottest, you get better and change the circumstances around you, letting yourself and those around you be lifted to a higher level?

You can be the kind of person who, through facing your life challenges together with God's love, enriches this world. and gives inspiration and help to others.

There is one more benefit to using this method. As I reveal on my retreats and in my book "The Fast Lane", I was a lost teenager. I sat alone in my high school cafeteria for four years. I wouldn't want to go back and relive those years, but I am glad they were a part of my life story. Since, with the love of God, I eventually changed, I have been able to help many people who also are isolated and lonely. I am able to spot the person, who is by themselves, and reach out to them, because I feel something of what they're going through. No matter what you will go through, someday you will meet someone you will be able to help through their challenge. It will be so because they will know from the way you speak and act towards them that you understand, because you have been there. This is another reason not to waste time and energy dwelling on the past and regretting.

You will have more to give, *not* less.

When you're born **you** are crying, and **everyone** around you is smiling.
Live your life in such a way so that at the end of your life the opposite happens.
That when you die **you're** smiling because you knew God and lived a blessed life, and **everyone** around you is crying because you loved them so much, and they'll miss you.

Whatever it is you are going through, *know that you will get through it. Not get over it, not get around it- through it.*

Building:
Read the Bible- it is filled with good advice and inspiration
Google the specific challenge you're going through for some practical tips
I invite you to check out my book "The Fast Lane." It is about the adventure of a life lived with God, and provides a lot of insights and inspiration to help you both get through life's challenges and live a new life in God's Holy Spirit.

     PS- I don't make any money on it. Any proceeds goes to Hope for the Children Foundation and helps the poor around the world.

A message to parents and adults working with youth.

This book is radical, because it puts God first, front, and center in the process of dealing with life's challenges. The most insidious form of child abuse is the neglect of a child's soul. It is the only part of who they are that will live forever. To live a soulless life is a living hell here on earth, and leaves the young ill-prepared to face life's challenges.

The young need so much more than just parents, teachers and church people, who are merely a little less crazy than the world at large.

They need to have people in their lives who are alive with the Holy Spirit.

You can make a child go to church every week, but if they never see a person who lives their life in a way that demonstrates they are animated by the spirit of God, they will never believe any of this is true.

We all need to look at what we are giving the young as an example. What will they come to believe about themselves and life; if when they see us adults, as we go through hard times, reach for a pill, or a bottle, or a cigarette, or we go shopping, or we lash out at strangers in our way?

Do they see us pray?

Do they see us offer up our hardships for the good of others?

Do they see us hold true to the high principles of love, even when our peers have abandoned them?

It's time to recognize that the spoiling of our children is doing exactly that. The child given everything, the very best as soon as they want it, grows up with no inner reserves for life. They grow up believing that everything comes to them; and then act in an infantile manner when it doesn't. The spoiled child has no use for God. In their eyes, mommy and daddy, or spoiling grandparents, coaches or teachers have become their gods. Some parents and adults want to give youth everything, making them completely dependent on them. They want to be God in the lives of the young.

      Children and teens don't need this. They don't need to be spoiled. They need people who will lead them to the truth: God is God, and not you. They need to be guided to find the inner reserves through their relationship with God that will enable them to face life's challenges.

Pray for the young
Tell them the truth
Model the truth;
that because Jesus is who He says He is, we must never lose hope or be crippled with fear. With the grace of God, there is nothing we cannot get through; and in the midst of a very challenging time we live in; in Christ's true peace, love, hope, freedom, courage, strength, dignity and integrity are possible.

> ***May you have***
> ***enough happiness***
> ***to have a gentle heart,***
> ***enough challenges***
> ***to make you strong,***
> ***enough sadness***
> ***to keep you human,***
> ***and enough hope***
> ***to make you happy.***

Tony Bellizzi is available for retreats and educational presentations including this DARE method

For more information/ booking:
visit HopefortheChildren.org or contact 718-479-2594

These spiritual growth tools by Tony Bellizzi are available
(amounts are suggested donations & includes postage)

Books

___DARE (Dealing with life's challenges)	$10.00
___The Fast Lane (Spirituality)	$12.00
___La Via Rapida ('The Fast Lane" in Spanish)	$10.00
___Living Bread (Eucharistic Miracles)	$10.00
___Full of Grace (Apparitions of Mary)	$10.00
___Mijo (Everyman's Journey)	$12.00
___Mijo (Spanish)	$12.00
___Amigo (Mijo companion journal)	$10.00
___The Civilization of Love	$10.00

Guided meditation CD's $10.00 each

___Journey with Jesus
___A Walk with Jesus
___A Special time with Jesus & Mary

Mail with Check made out to "Hope for the Children"
    9021 Springfield Blvd.   Queens Village NY 11428

Name_____

Address _____

City, State, Zip_____

Email_____Phone_____

Facebook_____